D1388032

79 533 499 7

·THE GOLDEN AGE OF·
BRITISH STEAM

·THE GOLDEN AGE OF·
BRITISH STEAM

JOHN WESTWOOD

WHSMITH
EXCLUSIVE
·BOOKS·

This edition produced exclusively for
W.H. Smith Ltd
Greenbridge Industrial Estate
Greenbridge Road
Swindon
Wiltshire SN3 3LD

Produced by
Bison Books Ltd
Kimbolton House
117A Fulham Road
London SW3 6RL

Copyright © 1991 Bison Books Ltd

All rights reserved. No part of this publication may
be reproduced, stored in a retrieval system or
transmitted in any form by any means, electronic,
mechanical, photocopying or otherwise, without first
obtaining the written permission of the copyright
owner.

ISBN 0-86124-822-8

Printed in Hong Kong

10 9 8 7 6 5 4 3 2 1

Overleaf: *One of the
surviving locomotives of
the Midland Railway, a
six-wheel design that was
used for both freight and
passenger work.*

Page 1: *An old LMS
Pacific steams out of
Stanforth Tunnel.*

Pages 2-3: *A classic
silhouette over
Headingley Viaduct,
Leeds.*

Below: The *Duchess of
Hamilton leaves Appleby.*

CONTENTS

THE SYSTEM AND THE SERVICE

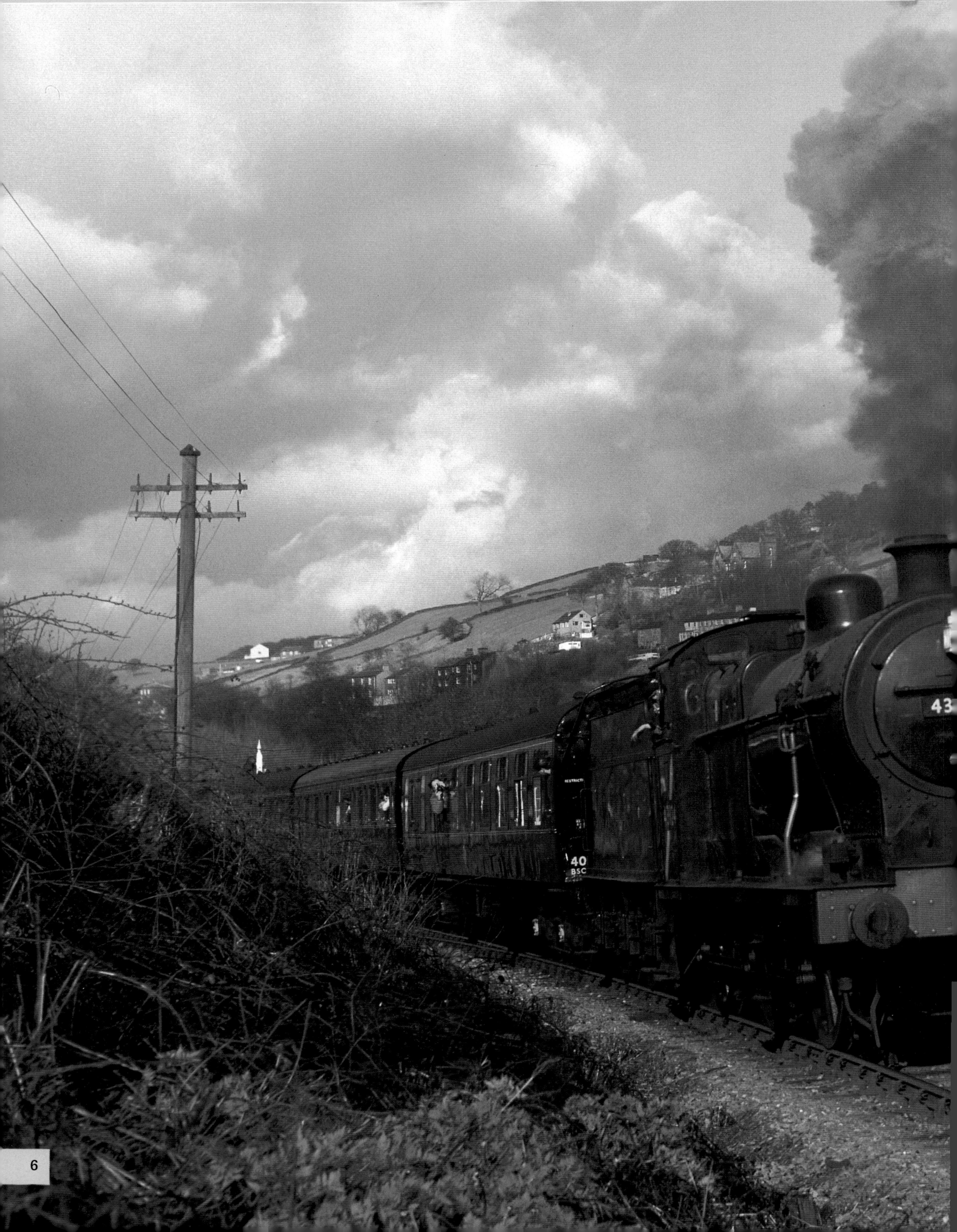

If there was a golden age for the British steam railway, it began around the turn of the century. But it derived its impetus from the last decade of the nineteenth century, a decade that witnessed a change of emphasis from expansion to improvement.

The last main line, the Great Central's grand but rather unnecessary route from Yorkshire through Leicester to London, was opened in 1899. That same decade had begun with the crossing of the last big water barrier with the completion of the Forth Bridge, and there had been some long lines built in the hope of opening up the Scottish Highlands. These included the spectacular West Highland Railway to Fort William, and a direct route to Inverness. But, henceforth, railways would be built not so much to develop new areas as to provide shortcuts for existing routes.

While the last routes were being built in the 1890s, some railway companies were setting the pattern for the following century by introducing improvements to reduce costs and attract more traffic.

In many cases such improvements were part of the competitive struggle between companies serving the same routes, but it is remarkable that several railway managements strove to improve their services even where they faced no competition. Imitation, perhaps spurred by a press that was interested in railways and never failed to make derogatory comparisons of one company with another, was a very potent motivation. It showed in the steady improvement of the facilities offered to third-class passengers: this was started by the Midland Railway in the 1870s and had spread in 1890 even to the traditionalist Great Western Railway, which opened all of its trains to third-class passengers. Fired perhaps by its own daring in making this leap, the GWR was itself soon among the most innovative of companies, and in 1892 introduced corridor trains; these, too, were soon imitated by other companies. For the average passenger, they were probably the most significant step forward in making railway travel a pleasurable experience.

Right: *A locomotive of the Great Southern Railways, formed to group the railways of the Irish Republic in 1925. It is a passenger 0-6-2 tank design introduced in 1933.*

Below right: *Darlington Station of the North Eastern Railway, in about 1887.*

Below: *The busy junction at Lewes on the London Brighton & South Coast Railway. On the right a London express, carrying distinctive LBSCR headcode, is taking water.*

The advances in technology and service achieved in the first 14 years of the twentieth century were so great as to constitute almost a revolution. And while these very fundamental and fascinating changes were taking place there was an almost equal fascination in the superficialities of the railway scene. The existence of almost 200 railway companies, each with its own peculiarities, was interesting not only for the growing band of railway enthusiasts but also for the public, and knowledge of

the railway system was a great social asset. At a time when there was a choice of route and company for most inter-city journeys, it was important to know which trains might possess a toilet, which companies were likely to be the most punctual, the most polite, the most clean, and the most thoughtful. (The Great Central, breaking belatedly into the London market, relied heavily on building a public reputation for all-round excellence. It succeeded in this endeavor, but never quite attracted enough

business to reward its ordinary shareholders). The seasoned traveler, or the attentive newspaper reader, would know this kind of detail, and moreover would be able to recognize trains of the different companies by their paintwork. Locomotives and coaches were painted in distinctive liveries that were not only ornate but painstakingly applied. Locomotives of the more prestigious companies might receive 14 or 15 coats in a repaint, so as to obtain the precise hue, the right depth, and the glossiest of finishes.

There were about a dozen great companies, a score of intermediate concerns, and the rest were short lines, usually allied to one of the bigger companies. The Irish railways were part of the British network and did not include any big companies, although two big English companies, the London and North Western and the Midland, owned or dominated lines in Ireland.

The LNWR was the second biggest of the companies in terms of route mileage, which was almost 2000 miles. It was descended from several of the Stephenson lines, notably the pioneer London & Birmingham, and Grand Junction railways. Its main line ran from a grandiose London terminus at Euston through the Midlands to its junction at Crewe, from where it had lines continuing to North Wales and

Holyhead, Liverpool and Manchester, and to Carlisle for an end-on link with one of the biggest Scottish companies, the Caledonian Railway. In its passage through Lancashire it had fairly amicable relations with the Lancashire and Yorkshire Railway, with which it merged in 1922.

The LNWR and CR formed the West Coast consortium for operating Anglo-Scottish services. The rival East Coast consortium consisted of three companies, the Great Northern which ran from London (Kings Cross) as far as Doncaster, the North Eastern from Doncaster to Berwick, and then the second of the big Scottish companies, the North British, to Edinburgh and beyond. In terms of route mileage, the NER at about 1700 miles was the third largest of the British companies.

A third Anglo-Scottish consortium had emerged in 1875, when the Midland Railway had opened its spectacular Settle & Carlisle line through the Pennines. Hitherto the MR had operated from its St Pancras terminus in London to Derby and Yorkshire, while also possessing a key cross-country route from Derby through Birmingham to Bristol. With the new line it could run to Carlisle, handing over its trains to Scottish companies for movement on to Glasgow and Edinburgh. It could never beat the older consortia on speed, so attracted passengers by superior comfort and stress on the scenic virtues of its route.

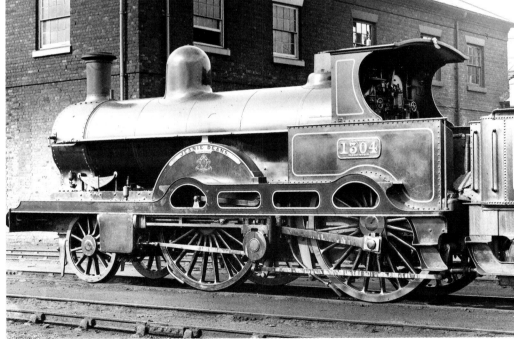

Far left above: *A Midland Railway 2-4-0 passenger locomotive in its maroon livery.*

Left: *Caledonian Railway 4-4-0 locomotives waiting to haul special holiday trains.*

Top: *A 'Single' of the 1890s hard at work on the Great Northern Railway main line.*

Above: *The London & North Western Railway's most celebrated compound locomotive, Jeanie Deans, a regular performer in the Anglo-Scottish service.*

The largest company, operating about 2500 miles of route, was the Great Western. Engineered by Isambard Brunel in the 1830s to connect London with Bristol, it was later extended to the West Country, Wales and the West Midlands. It had been a broad-gauge line, and the final conversion to standard-gauge had taken place only in 1892, when the last broad-gauge train left the London terminus at Paddington. It had been an exciting railway in its early decades, had then passed through an unenterprising phase, but by the 1890s was once more among the progressive companies. It had finally finished its Severn Tunnel in the 1880s, considerably accelerating its service to South Wales, and was seeking ways to compete on more favorable terms with the London & South Western between London and Devon, and the LNWR between London and Birmingham. Not for nothing was the GWR termed the 'Great Way Round' by its critics, and its lines from London to Devon (which passed via Bristol) and to Birmingham (via the Thames Valley) were plainly circuitous, a circumstance the Company had so far mitigated by high-speed running and above-aver-age comfort. In preparation for faster schedules, in the 1890s the GWR bought out at great expense the caterers at Swindon Station, who had an entrenched right to require that all trains stopped there for at least ten minutes in order that passengers might buy refreshments.

Of the several railways that titled themselves 'Great,' only the GWR seemed to have an unquestioned right to the description, although the Great Central was a strong candidate. The Great Eastern, with its dark blue and gilt passenger locomotives and its grand boat trains to Harwich, obviously had pretensions to greatness but, serving the mainly agricultural territory of East Anglia, it lacked the prosperity needed to buy its way into grandeur. The Great Northern had such prosperity, but lacked the pretensions. It was a businesslike railway centered on its London-Yorkshire main line and excelled in its engineering, but had no time for grand gestures. As for the Great North of Scotland, based on Aberdeen, and the two Irish companies Great Southern and Western, and Great Northern (Ireland), all three were really collections of long

Left: *A broad-gauge express of the Great Western Railway, running over mixed-gauge track. The widely spaced cylinders of the 'Single' locomotives are clearly visible.*

Above: *A 'Saint' 4-6-0 of the GWR passes over the roofs of Swansea.*

Right: *An LBSCR Pullman train, the 'Southern Belle,' built in 1908.*

Left: *A Great Northern 'Single', now preserved.*

Above: *A preserved Caledonian Railway 0-6-0 in the company's blue livery.*

Right: *Another Scottish 0-6-0:* Maude *of the North British Railway, one of several of its class given the names of First World War generals.*

branchlines and the first word of their respective titles could charitably be described as a triumph of dream over reality or, uncharitably, as an unprovoked assault on the public's credulity.

Most railways made most of their money from freight. Some, like the North Eastern or the small Taff Vale Railway in Wales, depended heavily on coal for their revenue. In southern England the balance was different, with passengers playing a far more important role. Of the southern companies, the London & South Western with its 850 miles of route stretching from London into Cornwall was certainly a mainline railway, whereas its neighbors to the east, the London Brighton & South Coast, and the South Eastern & Chatham were sometimes regarded (although not by themselves) as glorified suburban railways. The LSWR, in competition with the GWR for the Devon and Cornwall traffic, with the LBSCR for the Portsmouth, but having a virtual monopoly to Southampton and Bournemouth, was smartly run, but the same could not be said for the SECR. The latter was an alliance of two former rivals, the London Chatham & Dover and the South Eastern railways. Both cheaply built, they had for decades almost ruined themselves in unproductive beggar-my-neighbor competition. In so doing they had determined the railway geography of Kent, often to the disadvantage of that county. Possibly the duplication of cross-channel docks at Dover and Folkestone, and of different stations for the same destinations at Maidstone, Canterbury, and elsewhere were a sign of well-being, but if the companies had spent less of their money on competing facilities and more on decent trains to ride in, they would have been more popular in Kent. By 1899 everybody had had enough, and they decided to form a committee to run the two companies together, thereby giving birth to the SECR, which towards the end of its short life showed signs of making amends for past misdemeanors.

As for the LBSCR, this was virtually as much a territorial monopoly as the North Eastern or Lancashire and Yorkshire. But unlike those two, it was primarily a passenger line. Its prime route was the 51-mile line from its London terminus at Victoria to Brighton, and it ran a frequent service of smart trains, including Pullman services. Because so many of its routes were short, it was a great user of tank locomotives.

In Scotland the Caledonian and North British were dominant in the lowlands, with the Glasgow & South Western maintaining a foothold to Ayr and Stranraer. In the northern Highlands, the Highland Railway had a long singletrack main line from Perth through Inverness to the very top of Scotland at Thurso, over which its traffic was spread very thinly. Like its impecunious neighbor the Great North of

Scotland, it remained a territorial monopoly because it served a region whose traffic was barely enough for a single company. Just as the GNSR had its brief moments of glory because it served Balmoral, the HR enjoyed the grouse season. But in 1914 it became a line of national importance as it was the only railway within reach of the Grand Fleet base at Scapa Flow.

No company quite resembled another, and there was barely enough coordination between them to justify references to a British railway system. But Parliament had ensured that individualism would

Above: A special goods platform built by the Midland Railway for the Derby Royal Show of 1906, in which windmills were evidently a principal exhibit. A variety of vans are being unloaded, and an MR outside-frame 0-6-0 is busy on the left.

not be allowed to go to extremes. It was Parliament in 1850 that had formalized the Railway Clearing House, at which companies' representatives discussed matters arising out of through traffic traveling over more than one company's lines, and it was Parliament, through the Board of Trade, which supervised other matters requiring a nationwide approach. In 1889, the Regulation of Railways Act forced on to the railways essential safety standards that some companies had long resisted. Among these were an automatic brake for passenger trains, and the interlocking of signals so that one signal in-

dication could not conflict with another. But it is significant that the loophole left by the Act (it did not specify which kind of automatic brake) led to some companies investing in the vacuum brake, and others equipping themselves with the air brake, thereby restricting braked vehicles to those lines which used the same system.

But while it may be argued that the British companies did not constitute a genuine system, because they were not sufficiently standardized, there is no doubt that there was a true railway network. The railway map of 1914 showed a dense intertwining of

routes. Most of the arterial main lines started from London, but these were complemented by some heavy-traffic inter-city routes which came nowhere near the capital: the MR Derby-Bristol line, the Lancashire and Yorkshire's Manchester-Leeds trackage, and the competing routes between Edinburgh and Glasgow came into this category. Between the trunk lines came the secondary cross-country lines, and then there were the branches. Sometimes, as in Scotland, such branches could be long, but in the absence of motor transport there was also a place for the branch line of only a mile or two, serving a township that had not been favored with a main line. In England south of the Pennines almost everyone was within walking distance of a railway.

In 1888 the East and West coast consortia engaged in the so-called 'Race to Scotland,' a bout of competitive, almost day-to-day, schedule cutting which delighted all sections of the public except that section which actually used the trains in question. Fortunately there were no accidents, and, even more miraculously, nobody came to grief in the renewed outburst of speeding of 1895, the 'Race to Aberdeen.' However, the hell-for-leather competition between the GWR and LSWR boat trains from Plymouth to London, while it produced the record run of the GWR *City of Truro*, also led directly to the lethal Salisbury derailment on the LSWR. After this, the companies avoided any suggestion of 'racing,' but nevertheless continued to speed up their better trains partly to impress the public but partly, it would seem, to impress themselves as well; it is always difficult to resist the lure of advancing technology and this was a time when locomotive engineering, signaling systems, and track standards combined to make possible the running of trains

faster than had been seen previously. Part of the public, perhaps the most vociferous part and it included royalty, found high speed exciting, although there were still those who argued, logically enough, that if a train had an accident the consequences would be worse if it was traveling at high speed.

The railways themselves were ambivalent in their attitude towards faster trains. They appreciated the public enthusiasm for acceleration but would have preferred to operate their services at traditional speeds, except where competition spurred them on. The cost accountant was still a rarity in railway service, and the possibility of getting more daily mileage out of trains that moved faster was not appreciated. On the other hand, it seemed obvious that faster trains would lead to more wear and tear and hence higher costs. So most companies compromised by accelerating their better services but allowing the general run of trains to proceed at their traditional speed.

Top left: *The ornate coat of arms of the Midland Railway.*

Above: *A catastrophic collision on the NER at Castle Hill in 1894, between the Edinburgh-London night express and a local train.*

Upper right: *The NER coat of arms.*

Right: *The black LMS freight locomotive livery, worn by one of the Stanier '8F' locomotives.*

At the turn of the century the American and French railways provided more speed than the British. Indeed, if an average speed of 55 mph between stops was taken as the standard for fast trains, Britain had only five such services, three being on the Caledonian Railway, a line that was physically not the most suitable for high running speeds; the other two runs were on the Great Northern, a railway which certainly was suited to high speed, as subsequent decades would demonstrate.

It was the GWR which set the pace. After the death of Queen Victoria, high speed for royal trains was no longer frowned upon, and it was a GWR royal train that managed to cover the 194 miles from London to Exeter at an average of 67 mph in 1903. Competition for the Ocean Mail traffic from Plymouth spurred on the GWR, leading to the famous run of 9 May 1904 when *City of Truro* ran from Exeter to Bristol at 70 mph and was believed to have exceeded 100 mph at one point. Soon afterwards the GWR introduced two concepts that would guarantee its ability to run punctual, safe and fast trains for decades to come. Its locomotive superintendent, George Churchward, began to produce locomotives of a radically new design that were clearly superior to their predecessors, and the company also introduced what it called Automatic Train Control, a device that gave an audible indication to drivers of the aspect of an advance warning signal, and automatically applied the brake if it was at danger. In subsequent decades, as this ATC was extended, the

GWR not only became an exceptionally safe railway but also one on which trains tended to run to time in foggy weather. The failure of other companies to follow suit is interesting, and even more interesting is the failure of Parliament to compel them to do so.

One way of shortening schedules was to reduce the number of stops, and the nonstop train began to have a great appeal for the public. This was another of those advances which rested on technological change, for the long nonstop run depended on the corridor train, with its easy access to toilets and dining car, as well as on water troughs that enabled locomotives to take water at speed. Here again the GWR set the lead, for in the summer of 1904 it scheduled its 'Cornish Riviera Limited' from London to Plymouth, 246 miles, without a stop.

By 1914 all the big railways, except the North British, were operating trains that ran nonstop for 100 miles or more. The LNWR, with its long trunk lines, provided 41 such trains, followed by the GWR with 33, and even the Great Eastern managed seven. The London & South Western, with four, was at a disadvantage because it had no water troughs, but compensated for this by providing its principal passenger locomotives with massive eight-wheel high-capacity tenders.

By making the best trains nonstop, the companies automatically created a host of dissatisfied clients from intermediate stations no longer served by those trains. To some extent another new technology, the slip coach, came to the rescue of these deprived citizens. The slip coach was a vehicle that could be uncoupled from a moving train and conducted by its own impetus into the platform of an approaching station, a special guard being carried to operate its brake. In this way passengers were able to travel to stations at which their train was not scheduled to stop; they merely had to make sure they were sitting in the correct vehicle at, or towards, the rear of the train. The 'Cornish Riviera Limited' slipped coaches for the benefit of Taunton and Exeter passengers and, in later years, at Westbury. Other railways used them too. The cautious LNWR, aware of potential embarrassments, made sure that everything would be alright by employing horses to haul in the slip coach detached from its London – Birmingham trains at Coventry. Unfortunately, slip coaches could not be used to pick up passengers, although the technique of picking up mailbags at speed had long been mastered.

In the Edwardian years the GWR built itself three cut-off routes. One through Berkshire and Hampshire west of Reading enabled its Devon trains to avoid the circuitous route through Bristol, and thereby finally ended in the GWR's favor the competition with the LSWR for the best of the London – Plymouth traffic. Another, built to improve service and reduce costs, took trains direct from Swindon to the Severn Tunnel, avoiding the detour through Bristol. The third cut-off was a succession of short lines, some built in cooperation with the Great Central, that brought the GWR's London-Birmingham distance down to 110 miles, enabling the GWR to match the LNWR's timings. These companies soon ran two-hour trains between the two cities, but eventually came to an agreement that they would not cut schedules any further. Before 1914 the GWR also came to an understanding with the LSWR on the division of traffic between London and the West, while the East and West coast consortia agreed not to cut the daytime London-Edinburgh timing below eight and a quarter hours. By 1914, competitive schedule cutting was in decline, with companies preferring to reach understandings on speeds, and waging competition in other fields like comfort, punctuality and, increasingly, advertising.

The 44 miles between Darlington and York on the North Eastern Railway have always been regarded as ideal for high speed, with their flat and fairly straight alignment. In 1914 this stretch boasted Britain's fastest schedule, with one train averaging

Below: *A specialized terminal for perishables. This is a London depot of the Midland Railway at the turn of the century, when churns were used even for long-distance milk transport.*

Right: *On one of the last summer holidays before World War One, passengers embark at the GWR's Paddington Station in London.*

61 mph. But the Great Central also had a train making the same speed, which was hardly publicized at all because it was a newspaper train that happened to carry a few passengers. This was the 2.45 a.m. newspaper train from London, originally introduced to carry the *Daily Mail*, and which covered the Leicester to Nottingham sector at 61 mph. There were several railways that offered schedules of 55 mph or over, and this number included two unlikely performers, the once-ramshackle SECR and the single track heavily-graded Highland Railway. Ordinary trains were still rather slow, but in general were faster than corresponding trains in continental Europe or North America.

But while it was the passenger trains that interested the general public, the railways were equally interested in their freight traffic, and competition between companies was strong in some areas. There was a difference between those areas served by a single railway, as in the territories of the North Eastern, Great Eastern, Lancashire & Yorkshire and certain other companies, and those areas in which inter-company competition was strong. By far the most important freight was coal, carried mainly in wagons owned by the different coal com-

panies, and most mines were served by a single railway company. However, despite the absence of competition, railways serving the coal areas were often anxious to introduce new technology for the sake of cost reduction. The NER, serving the Yorkshire coalfields, was a pioneer in the introduction of high-capacity mineral wagons, while the Midland Railway introduced a form of centralized train control largely to cope with its coal traffic from the East Midlands to London. In South Wales, a number of small railway companies built lines up the valleys and developed a simple and effective service for getting loaded trains down to the docks and the empties back up the valleys again, using tank locomotives of the 0-6-2 wheel arrangement to cope with their short frequent trains over winding and heavily graded track.

It was in the other types of freight that the railways made their greatest sales effort, however. Bulk freight was largely captive freight and traveled at low rates, whereas merchandise, which was mainly high-value finished products moving in small consignments at high tariffs, was fought for. Traders were wooed by the companies with all kinds of privileges, whose true costs the railways probably did

FOR PARTICULARS OF

FACTORY SITES
OR VACANT PREMISES ON THE L·N·E·R SYSTEM IN ENGLAND OR SCOTLAND APPLY TO
THE INDUSTRIAL AGENT
KING'S CROSS STATION   LONDON N1
TELEPHONE TERMINUS 4200   EXTENSION 3396

fresh fish from Grimsby or Fleetwood, fresh beef from the Highlands and, conversely, for non-Londoners to consume fresh newspapers from London.

Quite apart from merchandise vehicles running almost empty, empty freightcar mileage was enormous and wasteful. Under the old companies, an unloaded freightcar not belonging to the destination railway had to be sent straight back to the owning railway, which meant that it was usually sent back empty. The pooling of freightcars, so that a consignment could be taken by the first available empty car, would have brought great economies, but it was only when the railways came under government control in World War One that hesitant steps were taken in this direction, the first move being made in 1915 when three railways (GCR, GER, GNR) agreed to pool their open wagons. Gradually, during and after the war, more companies and more vehicle types were included, but it was not until World War Two that the process was concluded, with specialized vehicles like meat and fruit vans being brought into the scheme.

The centralized control of the railways in World War One brought increased efficiency, and it was generally agreed that a return to a network divided between almost 200 companies would be a step backward. After the war, government control continued while the shape of a future railway organization was discussed, both by Parliament and by the public in general. Outright nationalization was ruled out, and a system divided between a few large companies was favored, it being thought that this would offer the advantages both of competition and of size.

Eventually, the option of a separate company for Scotland having been rejected, Parliament approved a railway amalgamation that created, in 1923, four new companies by grouping all but the smallest of the older companies. The GWR remained more or less as it was, but absorbed lines in central and south Wales and became the third largest of the new companies at 3700 miles. The smallest of the new companies was the Southern Railway, an amalgamation of the London & South Western, the SECR, and the LBSCR, totalling 2100 miles. The biggest, the London Midland & Scottish, was an uneasy combination of companies that had not always been very friendly in the past: the London & North Western, Midland, Caledonian, Highland, and Glasgow & South Western railways, together with the rather smaller Furness Railway and the North Staffordshire. It also included the Lancashire & Yorkshire, one of the most progressive companies that had amalgamated with the LNWR a few months earlier. The LMS had over 7000 miles of route and passed through some of the most heavily industrialized areas of the country. The second largest company,

Left: The LNER advertises available factory sites. By offering favorable terms, companies could attract new factories, and hence new freight, to their territory.

Right: A Beyer-Garratt locomotive of the LMS doing the work for which it was designed, hauling coal trains between Nottinghamshire and London.

Below: An LNER 2-6-0 at work on former North British Railway territory in Fifeshire.

not realize. Railway freightcars would rest for days or even weeks on sidings so that merchants could use them as warehouses. Managements made careful and successful arrangements so that any small consignment left at any small freight station would be promptly picked up by a local freight train, transferred to another, longer-distance train and be delivered to the consignee the very next day. This complex arrangement was admirable, but it meant that the railways, which by nature were bulk carriers, dissipated their resources. To the hidden cost of vehicles used as warehouses had to be added the thousands of freightcars that crossed the country loaded only to a quarter or less of their capacity.

At the same time, the technological level was low, with freightcars of small capacity, coupled by loose chains, and without brakes that could be operated while in motion. Competition for merchandise traffic did at least compel the companies to modernize a part of their freight rolling stock with vehicles that were continuously braked and tightly coupled. The scheduled fast freight train appeared, often running at night to ensure the advertised next-morning delivery, and such trains were a credit to the companies that operated them, as well as an asset for the public. It was such trains that enabled, for example, the Londoner to consume fresh milk from Devon,

at about 6300 miles, was the London & North Eastern, which took over the Great Northern, Great Eastern, Great Central, North Eastern, North British and Great North of Scotland companies. Some of these were barely able to make ends meet, but it was hoped that the strong North Eastern would provide financial strength for the new company, a hope that was dashed when the coal industry entered its inter-war depression.

The four new companies settled down at different speeds. The Great Western had no problems; it already had close relations with the smaller railways it had absorbed. The Southern Railway, which might have been expected to have problems, since it contained the unpopular SECR, also came out well because its new general manager, Herbert Walker from the LSWR, was a gifted man who soon had his departments working as a team. The London & North Eastern, partly because it did not have the funds to spend on standardization, let the old company managements carry on very much as before, but under different names, and only slowly did a corporate image emerge. It was the London Midland and Scottish Railway which had real problems. Of its constituent companies, the Caledonian and Glasgow & South Western were at daggers-drawn, the Midland felt it knew all the answers, and the LNWR really did believe that it was the 'Premier Line' even though by 1923 it was old-fashioned in many ways. Moreover, inside the LNWR was a progressive group of managers who had come from the recently-absorbed Lancashire & Yorkshire. In the new LMS men of the old companies, instead of merging into a new team, continued to pursue the old rivalries and endeavored to impose their methods as the standard of the new, bigger, LMS. A concrete manifestation of this continual battle was the new design of 2-6-0 locomotive produced by the LMS, whose front half was clearly L & Y in inspiration, and whose rear half was pure Midland. It was not until the LMS brought in from Imperial Chemical Industries a new general manager, Josiah Stamp, that the requisite strong measures were taken to weld the new company, like it or not, into a coordinated and forward-looking whole.

The government had never fulfilled its wartime promise of recompensing the railways for the heavy traffic and delayed maintenance of the war years, but it was inertia rather than run-down facilities that caused the new companies to neglect passenger train acceleration. The motor car and the motor coach were still in their infancy, and there was no statistical evidence that higher speeds would attract more passengers. Even by 1929 average speeds on the LMS and LNER were still slightly slower than in 1914, and on the GWR and SR slightly higher, so the national average was about one per cent slower than before the war. On the other hand, the average train was slightly more comfortable, thanks to the progressive replacement of old rolling stock, and trains were more frequent. For the passenger greater train frequency represented, quite often, a considerable saving of time even though the trains might be slower.

In the 1930s speed increased markedly, the comparatively few record-breaking trains encouraging a more modest acceleration of the less spectacular long-distance services. The GWR 'Cheltenham Flyer' was the first of the fast trains scheduled largely to capture public attention. Running (in one direction only) a very tight schedule over the 77 miles from Swindon to London, it was timetabled to average 66 mph in 1929 and 71 mph in 1932, and on one day in 1932 covered the distance at an average of almost 82 mph.

After this, attention shifted to the Anglo-Scottish services, where the LMS and LNER, inheritors respectively of the West Coast and East Coast consortia, engaged in a contest that may have been less brash than the 'Race to Scotland' of 1895, but was certainly as impressive in engineering terms. This new competition was probably delayed by the inability of the LMS to provide suitable locomotives, and in the meantime the LNER practiced high-speed running with its 'Silver Jubilee,' introduced between London and Newcastle in 1935. Britain's first streamlined train, it was hauled by the new streamlined Pacific locomotives, and averaged 70 mph over the 232 miles between Darlington and London.

The 'Silver Jubilee' won the LNER enormous public prestige at a relatively small cost, so it was decided to repeat the success in 1937 by introducing two more such trains, the 'West Riding Limited' between London and Leeds, and the 'Coronation' between London and Edinburgh. The proposed six hour timing of the latter broke the old understanding that daytime London-Edinburgh services would not be scheduled at less than eight-and-a-quarter hours, a limitation observed by the existing top trains on this route, the LNER 'Flying Scotsman' and the LMS 'Royal Scot.'

The LMS decided that the time had come to show what it could do, although in the end its new 'Coronation Scot,' introduced in 1937, made the London to Glasgow run in six-and-a-half rather than six hours. It was a heavy train and traveled, in its northern half, a heavily graded route. Moreover, it attracted a full load of passengers in any case, the LMS management argued, so an even higher speed would merely raise operating costs without attracting extra revenue. In the interwar years, therefore, it was the LNER which won the reputation for operating the fastest trains.

The LNER trains, being specially designed, were also the most distinctive and probably the most comfortable. But for comfort they were at least equaled by the few Pullman services operated in Britain. Most of these were offered by the Southern Railway, whose constituent companies, LBSCR and SECR, had used them before the railway grouping. The 'Golden Arrow' London – Paris service, and the 'Brighton Belle' and 'Bournemouth Belle' were the best-known of these, and their soft chairs, table service at every seat, and at-your-elbow service attracted a sufficient number of passengers willing to pay the Pullman supplement to make such trains viable. The LNER also ran a handful of Pullman trains; the 'Harrogate Pullman,' which later became the 'Queen of Scots,' was one of these. It ran between London and Edinburgh through Harrogate and Newcastle and, with such circuitous routing, could not hope to provide a competitive schedule between the two capitals. But many passengers chose it, evidence that they were willing to exchange speed for comfort. The 'Yorkshire Pullman' to Hull was also a popular train. The other two companies did not favor the idea. The GWR went as far as introducing its 'Torquay Pullman,' but it did not long survive and the GWR, like the LMS, soon lost interest in the Pullman concept.

High-speed and luxury trains were of interest to only a small proportion of the passengers, and to increase passenger revenue the companies needed to adopt measures to make people want to travel more often by rail. Cheap excursions, running on particu-

Above: *Design compromise or power struggle in the new LMS? The 1926 2-6-0 with its Lancashire & Yorkshire-style front end and its ill-fitting Midland Railway tender reflects the conflict of engineering styles that beset the new Company's locomotive department.*

Upper left: *One of the few locomotives of the North Staffordshire Railway, an 0-6-2 tank design.*

Lower left: *A suburban train leaves Edinburgh, hauled by a 2-6-2 tank locomotive designed by Gresley for the LNER.*

lar days to particular destinations, were one increasingly used device, and so was the development of holiday traffic by advertising and better train service. Road competition had little effect on long-distance rail services because, thanks to the state of the roads, neither private car nor coach could match the train's speed.

Nevertheless, in the unstable economic situation between the wars there were years in which passenger traffic fell and, after much initial doubt, the railways finally responded by what in effect were reduced fares. What they did was to take existing cheap-fare concessions and extend their validity. Weekend tickets, which were return tickets priced at one third more than the single fare, became summer return tickets and were valid for a month. They soon became all-year tickets, known as monthly returns; for nine-tenths of the long-distance passengers, fares had been reduced to just a penny a mile.

Third-class passengers benefited in other ways. In 1928 the companies agreed that third class passengers could be offered sleeping accommodation, and all companies except the SR thereupon built coaches with four-berth compartments provided

Above: *The famous Flying Scotsman of the LNER a Gresley Pacific designed in the Great Northern Railway tradition.*

Top right: Green Arrow, *a 'V2' mixed-traffic locomotive of the LNER which was a scaled-down version of the Gresley Pacific.*

with pillows and blankets (but not sheets). More restaurant cars were provided, and the cheaper buffet car made an appearance. But the companies could not agree on how many passengers a third-class compartment should seat. The essential problem was that the maximum width of vehicle permitted a side-corridor and a seat that could take four passengers tightly or three comfortably. The LMS and LNER decided to tackle this problem by fitting two movable armrests so that the seat was divided into three sections. They argued that if a train was crowded, passengers could lift up the armrests

and thereby increase capacity by 33 percent. In reality, unassertive British social behavior turned this expectation into a failed dream: passengers who needed a seat were too shy to ask and passengers who had a seat were too shy to offer. The GWR and SR stayed with four-a-side seating, tolerable when people were wearing summer clothes and were not too stout, but cramped otherwise.

Road competition made itself felt first in freight transport. The General Strike of 1926, which showed that road transport companies could haul much of the traffic hitherto regarded as a railway preserve, was a turning point. By the late 1920s the railways were seriously concerned about this, especially the LNER, which derived three-fifths of its revenue from freight, in contrast to the SR whose proportion was only one-quarter. Much of the railways' defensive stance rested on political action, culminating in a 'Square Deal!' campaign designed to equalize the statutory burdens of rail and road transport. But there were also attempts to provide a more competitive service. To match the door-to-door service of the highway operators, the railways introduced containers (whose competitive essence they unfortunately diluted by charging a supplement for their use), and provided more and faster regular express goods trains. Since the road companies attacked the most lucrative traffic, this emphasis on fast freights was rational, as high-value merchandise required fast, reliable and regular delivery. The GWR, meanwhile, was attempting to rationalize its local freight stations, placing itself 30 years ahead of its time by concentrating collection and delivery at a few centers in each district. The GWR's willingness to use road transport to move freight, when necessary, between nearby centers showed that its management had a clear appreciation of how an integrated transport system might work. Its successor, the British Transport Commission, never achieved this.

Previous pages: *The Midland Railway opens its Nottingham station in 1839. To modern eyes there is a sharp contrast between the grand station and the puny train, but that is not how contemporaries saw it.*

Left: *The three companies of the East Coast consortium advertise their service, with the aim of attracting potential passengers from the rival West Coast route.*

By about 1835 people were aware that the railway was not merely the promising novelty it had seemed a decade previously, but was a technical revolution that might bring with it a social revolution, although those were not the terms they used. They related what was happening to their own lives, and they foresaw that the railway was unstoppable, would spread, and would bring them benefits. By 1850 this conclusion had been confirmed, for the future main lines of the railway network had by then already been built, or at least were embodied in schemes approved by Parliament.

In this early period the press, which at that time was not a popular press, was full of railway news, but it tended to concentrate on railway-building schemes and on questions of finance. Only later would it become a grumbling ground for those who thought the railways were badly managed, or miserly, or greedy. However, artists and engravers were busy depicting railway scenes, and this pre-1850 period was perhaps more productive of such scenes than succeeding decades. The Stockton & Darlington and Liverpool & Manchester lines received a full share of attention, and indeed lithographs and paintings of that period are still used to illustrate railway history books. For some reason, however, the railways did not attract the great novelists or, rather, the railways when mentioned at all were part of the background rather than the skeleton of a plot.

By the end of the century the public was subjected to a rather different artistic treatment of the railways. In the realm of painting, the emphasis changed from depiction of railways to the treatment of people using the railways. When trains did form the main subject, they were usually to be found in the work of artists practising new styles and grateful for the atmospherics or angles that the railway scene could provide. Frith's famous 1863 painting of the platform scene at Paddington Station may be seen as a halfway stage in the process of moving from train to passenger. Paintings of passengers inside trains became a favorite, and the sentimentality which seemed to appeal to so many late Victorians and Edwardians could easily be aroused by pictures that busied themselves around the themes of partings, of unknown destinations, of embarrassing situations. The line between sentimentality and poignancy is very thin, and several paintings showing the departure of troops for war, whether to the Crimea or the Western Front, are still moving for modern generations, and moreover confirm how central was the railway to the lives of ordinary people. Despite the existence of three passenger classes, the railway station was a place in common, where everybody went, sharing the same problems and the same excitements.

The passenger classes were not as socially divisive as is sometimes imagined. True, the rich invari-

Above: *W P Frith's celebrated painting of the GWR at Paddington in broad-gauge days. The arrest of a criminal at the right is an event taken from life; a fleeing muderer intercepted at Paddington was the first to be caught with the aid of the railway telegraph. At this time (1863) luggage was still carried on the train roof.*

The Pleasures of the Rail-Road. — Caught in the Railway !

ably traveled first-class and the really poor third-class. But the mass of travellers came between the two extremes, and this mass did not regard itself as strictly first, second or third. It was quite common to travel part of the way in one class and part in another. There were several reasons for this (one was that one railway's third-class was as good as another's second), but if passengers were expecting to be met on arrival they quite commonly traveled second or third for most of the way and then, at the last change of train, moved into first-class for a dignified arrival.

One kind of artist, the cartoonist, found railways a rich source, and indeed this situation has continued right up to the present time. The railway, with its variety of subjects and backgrounds and its necessarily hierarchical and rigidly organized system, produced a rich crop of absurdities. Comic writers similarly took advantage of this situation. However, although great talent, and sometimes near-genius, was occasionally deployed on satirical or outraged comment about the railways, all too often the humorists concentrated on superficial

absurdities (which on closer examination might have been found to be perfectly reasonable) and did not dig deep enough to expose fundamental irrationalities and wrongs.

Probably the first big issue lending itself to satirical or critical treatment was the GWR's broad gauge and the inconveniences, real or imagined, that it occasioned. This is a good example of the superficial receiving more attention than the substantial, and the reason is plain. It was far easier for a satirist and, especially, the cartoonist, to portray a familiar detail, like the potentially hilarious shifting of cattle from broad to narrow-gauge vehicles, than it was to show the economic and technical arguments on this subject. There was nothing reprehensible in this. It was a case of good clean fun which did at least place itself on the side of the railways' sometimes neglected clients. At other times during the nineteenth century there were outbursts of complaint and blame that were justified and must have encouraged managements to make long-overdue changes. The outcry about train brakes following the Armagh accident in 1889 was one of those

Above: *A Henry Heath cartoon of 1831, depicting the fantastic perils of the new form of transport. Stephenson's* Northumbrian, *the first locomotive with an internal firebox, is drawn quite accurately.*

Tharpshecter, fec.

London: Sub. by G. Humphrey, 24, St James's Street, August 28, 1829.

PAT's COMMENT ON STEAM ENGINES.

By-and-bye a Man will go a hunting after breakfast upon his Tay-kettle.

Above: Another early cartoon, in which accuracy is joyfully jettisoned in the interest of whimsy and which, in the final analysis, is quite devoid of any message.

occasions, and sporadic concern about railwaymen's long working hours (often set off by anonymous railwaymen writing letters to their local newspaper) was also a positive contribution. In both these examples the public concern was transformed into parliamentary action.

But sniping at the railways also had a more sinister aspect, with perfectly sound managerial decisions being subjected to a barrage of press abuse that often reflected the interests not of the public but of a particular interest group. Harmful and unjustified distortion of reality was frequent. For example, there was the North Eastern Railway, a coal-hauling company that in many ways was one of the most efficient in Britain, being a proponent of bigger freight vehicles and the first to use a respectable statistical service. The NER did have a territorial monopoly in much of Yorkshire, but took great care to avoid accusations of monopolistic practices. Despite this, it suffered repeated and bitter attack from public figures and newspapers, especially in Hull. The source of these attacks was not devoted defenders of the public interest, but powerful members of the Hull Corporation, influenced by shippers aggrieved that the NER (which tried hard to be fair) was not offering them the low freight rates to which they felt entitled. In the end the NER's enemies succeeded in getting a second railway built to serve Hull. This was the Hull & Barnsley Railway which, as might have been expected, was an abject financial failure and was eventually merged with its intended victim the NER. When the large-scale closure of railways began in the 1960s, the former H & B lines were among the first to go. They were a good example of the mis-investment that can follow a successful twisting of public opinion.

Another, almost classic, sectional-interest campaign was launched against the newly-formed Southern Railway in the 1920s. One advantage of the railway grouping, it had been claimed, was that duplication of services characteristic of competition under the old companies could be eliminated. The SR, taking this seriously, soon set about redesigning the service between London and Portsmouth. Previously the LBSCR and LSWR had operated rival services, but the SR management decided that the fast trains over the LBSCR route could well be withdrawn. However, this route passed through terrain which, although not densely populated, was the home of many of Britain's loudest voices. Arundel had its duke, Chichester its bishop, and the smaller stations served the homes of important commercial and political figures. This was enough to sustain a campaign strong enough to persuade the SR to change its mind.

It was probably the last quarter of the nineteenth century that witnessed a subtle but far-reaching change in the relationship between railways and public or, more exactly, between railways and politics. It is interesting that the concept of the railway as primarily a public service developed, under the pressure of public opinion, at a period when railways were ostensibly a textbook example of profit-making capitalist organization. This concept, coupled with the tendency of managers to do the best that was technically possible without paying too much attention to real costs, meant that the balance between profitability and service increasingly favored service. Moreover, companies were not as free to make decisions as appeared. Agitation by outside interests, rightly or wrongly alleging that railway 'monopolies' had them at their mercy, led to 1888 legislation giving Parliament the final say over railway charges. A company which does not have control over its prices is not one which is likely to flourish in the long term, and political control over fares and freight tariffs was certainly a factor in the railways' relative commercial decline in the interwar years. But another way of looking at this situation would be to acknowledge that from the late nineteenth century the British public wanted railways to pay less attention to the pursuit of profits and more to the provision of public services.

The preference of press commentators for the quick laugh or the easy indignation rather than well thought-out, well researched, criticism that might have stimulated managements to do better, is well exemplified by the experience of British Railways. After December 31 1947 the railways were no longer private companies but a nationalized undertaking, an undertaking that was essentially socialist in concept operating in a country where the bulk of the newspapers were against socialism and against nationalization. In the following years press comment about the railways was savage, unfair, and ultimately harmful. Even when the railways did well they were criticized; indeed they did well to operate a service at all in conditions where wartime neglect had not been made good, where dedicated labor was hard to recruit, where capital investment was strictly limited and controled, where they had incomplete control over their charges, and where the sacred cow of the economy was the motor industry.

It was all very well to make jokes about the railway sandwich (indeed, this was one of those cases where press criticism might have brought a necessary improvement), but ceaseless complaints about late trains at a time when there were fundamental reasons why a better service could not be offered served only to intensify the bitterness of both railway users and railway operators. The latter were well aware that the press did not subject other forms of transport to the same criticism.

But at least the railways, from about the 1880s, had begun to learn the hard way about public relations and effective advertising. In fact the very term 'public relations' seems to have originated on the Southern Railway in the 1920s. Advertising, and influencing public opinion, had accompanied the railway age from the very beginning, but in the first decades had concentrated, on the one hand, on making services known to the public, and on the other on promoting the interests of one company against another in the struggle for new lines. There was little that was notable in these early efforts, although attracting prominent and therefore newsworthy people to railway-opening ceremonies (the Liverpool & Manchester even succeeded in getting the Duke of Wellington to come along) was a foretaste of a common twentieth century public relations technique, and the sponsorship by several

Upper right: *Back and front of a West Coast Route advertising card, published shortly before World War One.*

Center right: *A travel agent's stock-in-trade, with 'Bradshaw' ready for action.*

Far right: *A GWR timetable map. If space had been available, a GWR route to Vladivostok would no dount have been shown.*

Below: *An advertising postcard given away by the LNWR freight department and showing the express locomotive* Greater Britain, *which had been transferred to freight service.*

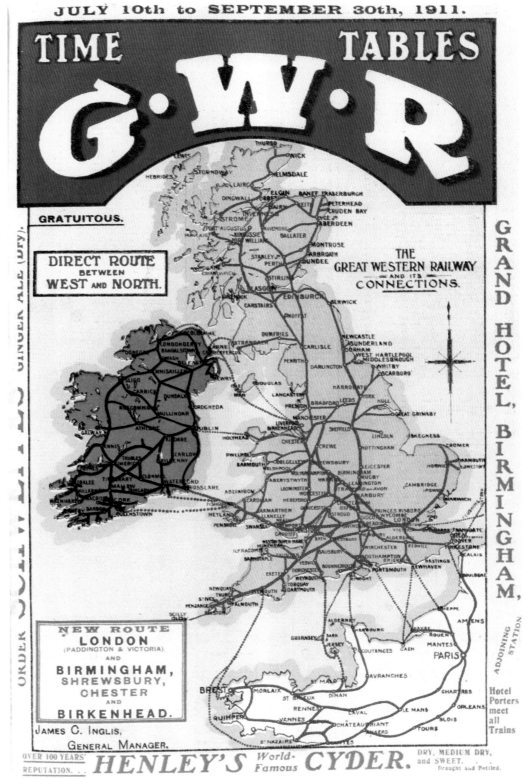

Left: *Not so much a nameplate as exterior decoration; the insignia of* Silver Fox, *the fourth of Gresley's streamlined Pacifics, is studied by the Kings Cross stationmaster.*

companies of guidebooks for the districts served by their lines was an endeavor that combined a useful public service with not only an advertisement of services but also a temptation to use them.

In the late nineteenth century the advertising slogan appeared. Here, again, the railways were the leaders of a new craft. The Midland Railway's punchline was 'The Best Way,' which gained currency more by constant repetition than by any recognizable authenticity. Far more effective, at the beginning of the new century, was the Lancashire & Yorkshire's 'On Time!' and this was all the more powerful because it was used to advertise a real improvement in punctuality laboriosly achieved by the L & Y management. The practice of conducting campaigns to neutralize justified criticism was not favored by the railways at that time nor, in general, in later years. However, the railways were not averse to a little deception in their publicity maps, although the sleight of hand was so obvious as to be something of a joke to all but the most credulous. These maps as a matter of course straightened out lines that would otherwise have seemed too roundabout, and claimed as company routes lines of other railways which ran in connection. More than one of the southern companies seemed to lay claim to a line serving Paris. The GWR map that for decades was framed in compartments of its trains was skilfully distorted (ostensibly so that it could fit into the narrow rectangular frame) so as to suggest that the territory served by the Company constituted three

quarters of Britain. The GER map that showed its meandering route from London to York as a determined straight line was perhaps one of the simplest and greatest achievements in the craft of railway map-making.

The railway poster varied from company to company. Scenes showing resorts served by the railway were typical, and pictures of the railway at work were at first rare. But the LMS in the 1920s did show railwaymen at work, and in World War Two the four companies exhibited 'The Lines behind the Lines' series, which put emphasis on the daily life of the railways. After the war this theme was combined with a certain romanticism, typified by Terence Cuneo's posters, which usually managed to combine the special attraction of steam power with an impression of the hard and intelligent work that was needed to keep a railway going.

After the railway grouping the four new companies entered a new, more professional, stage in their public relations. What is interesting is that although all four had the common objective of creating a favorable public image, each went about this task in a different way. The most modern in approach was the Southern Railway, which in the 1920s was assailed by press and public for the allegedly incompetent and uncaring way in which it operated its passenger trains into London. Commuters of the southern counties have traditionally been the most demanding of the railways' clients, often unreasonably so, and this campaign was all

the more deplorable because the SR was trying hard, and slowly succeeding, in improving the services it had inherited from its constituent companies. It was the unfairness of the criticism, which seemed likely to discourage the SR management and staff from further efforts, that prompted the appointment of a well-known journalist, John Elliot, to handle the situation. At Elliot's suggestion his job title became Assistant for Public Relations, and the appointment was an enormous success. The press changed its tone, appreciating this obvious endeavor to meet it halfway by providing, rather than hiding, all non-sensitive information. Henceforth train delays due to electrification work were portrayed as necessary sacrifices for the public good rather than as the result of culpable negligence on the part of the management. Aided by a series of appealing posters, a new architectural style, and other changes, the SR's public relations effort was highly successful because it rested not only on Elliot's skill but also on real achievements. By the 1930s the SR was probably the most popular of the four companies. Its posters seemed perhaps a trifle crude when compared to the paintings by Royal Acade-

Below: *The GWR used state-of-the-art technology to gets its message across.*

micians used by other companies, but they appealed to the common man, were catchy, and were forerunners of the robust style that became popular in Britain in the 1940s.

The SR had an additional publicity task, that of helping to unify the new company, and this was largely a question of internally-directed publicity. An effort was made to avoid imposing the practice of any one of the constituent companies as standard for the new company: the preference was to develop a new Southern style (an exception was the wearing

"THE CORONATION"
ON THE EAST COAST ENTERING SCOTLAND
IT'S QUICKER BY RAIL
FULL INFORMATION FROM ANY L·N·E·R OFFICE OR AGENCY

Upper left: *SR publicity: St Lawrence College boys visit 'Schools' class locomotive St Lawrence.*

Top center: *A 'Schools' class nameplate.*

Left: *A 1930s LNER poster by Frank Mason.*

favored the idea. However, it was a great success for the SR, and later passenger locomotives were also named.

Naming of locomotives had been quite common in the early railway age, being one of many features carried over from the stage coaches, but the practice had died out on many railways. The LNWR was among those which favored it, and tended to choose quite grandiose names, usually connected with history, for its engines. In Scotland the North British and Highland railways retained the practice, although they preferred the cheap method of paint or transfer for putting the name on the driving wheel splasher. Interestingly, it was the impecunious Great North of Scotland that shamed its neighbors by going to the expense of making brass nameplates. These were rather thin, somewhat like the LNWR pattern, but provided greater dignity.

Inevitably, it was not long before names of living people were chosen, a powerful form of flattery. Directors of a railway company were sometimes honored this way: even as late as the 1940s the LNER turned out a batch of B1 4-6-0s named after its directors. Other members of this class had been named after antelopes, which was not a good idea for a class destined to total more than 400 units. The LNER had already produced some strange names by commemorating successful racehorses, and ob-

of LSWR-issue red ties by workers, on the underlying assumption that such ties could be ripped off in emergencies to serve as red flags). In the mid-1920s the convention of referring to the South Western, Brighton and South Eastern sections of the SR was dropped, and a curtain wall dividing the former LBSCR and SECR stations at Victoria was pierced in order to form one unified station.

As a publicity move, Elliot recommended, among many other things, giving names to SR passenger locomotives. The choice of names from legends commemorating the mythical deeds of King Arthur's Knights for the leading 4-6-0 type was very apt for a railway serving Cornwall. Although the LBSCR had dabbled in locomotive names, usually painted on the side rather than displayed on nameplates, the other constituent railways had not

Above: A stylishly fashionable LNER poster of 1930.

Right: One of the last posters issued by the SECR, and typical of many aimed at potential exhibition visitors.

Left center: One of a long series of GWR posters depicting holiday destinations.

Left: *The publicity-conscious LNER puts its latest equipment on exhibition.*

Above: *Like its predecessor the North British Railway, the LNER took characters from Scott's novels as names for some of its locomotives designed for Scottish service.*

Right: *The GWR 'Star' class* Knight of Liège, *which before the German invasion of Belgium in 1914 was named* Knight of the Black Eagle, *a Prussian title.*

for service in central Wales. The earls were not amused, and the nameplates were rapidly transferred to new 'Castle' class locomotives. This was not the first time that GWR names had encountered difficulties. Earlier, a series of locomotives had been graced with names of towns served by the Company, but these nameplates had to be removed because too many passengers realized too late that the name of the engine was not the destination of the train. Several of the 'Star' class had to be renamed; when the Germans invaded Belgium in 1914, the Germanic *Knight of the Black Eagle* was quickly renamed *Knight of Liège*, and in World War Two, after the surrender of Belgium, *Belgian Monarch* lost its name, although the LNWR's *Queen of the Belgians* was untouched. The GWR chose names of country residences for most of its interwar series of

viously a company that could name its Pacifics *Spearmint* and *Pretty Polly* would not shrink from *Bongo* and *Kudu* for its 4-6-0s, but in the end most of the B1s were unnamed. As for naming engines after living people, it might have been expected that this practice would have disappeared in the 1930s, after the GWR mechanical department had disgraced itself in a comedy of its own making. Faced with a request to honor earls with GWR connections by according their names to new engines, Swindon chose to attach the appropriate nameplates to a batch of engines built to a small and obsolete design

4-6-0, the 'Castles,' 'Halls,' 'Granges,' and 'Manors' being each a distinct type. The hundreds of 'Hall' names were somewhat tedious; moreover, towards the end the barrel had to be scraped for new names, and one locomotive was inadvertently given the name of a Borstal institution. But whatever the shortcomings of the GWR choices of names, there was no doubt that its nameplates were the grandest. At the turn of the century it was using rather mean combined name and number plates, oval fitments on the cabside, but it soon changed to large nameplates mounted (not merely attached) on the central

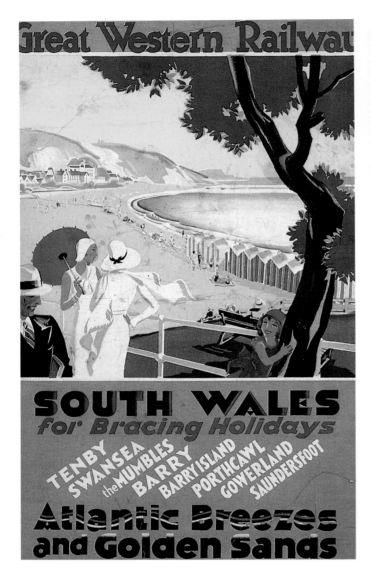

splasher on each side, the steel nameplate being of considerably larger diameter than the wheel and bearing the name in individual brass letters.

These huge and expensive nameplates were a true reflection of the GWR's corporate personality. In the interwar years it enjoyed great respect, achieved by means quite different from those of the SR. It had the advantage of retaining its name through the railway grouping, and it was a name well-known to the public. It skilfully, but as a matter of course rather than as an obvious campaign, drew on the accumulated folk memory of Brunel and the broad gauge, the Severn Tunnel epic, and the high quality of its engineering to create a picture of a company that was traditional in its outlook yet always ready to try out new ideas. The emphasis on tradition was seen in the reversion to its old passenger train livery of chocolate and cream, that had been abandoned for a less attractive all-over maroon before World War One. It developed a series of publications about its trains and locomotives, frankly aimed at 'boys of all ages,' providing technical information that hitherto had not been easily available to the public, while subtly implying that GWR technology was superior (as indeed it was in most respects). It soon found in the 'Cheltenham Flyer' an excellent means of staying in the news; excellent because journalists loved

record-breakers and because it hardly cost the Company a penny. The GWR had to run the train anyway, and timetabling a record average speed for less than 80 miles on a falling gradient could be done simply for the price of a few extra pounds of coal.

The LNER was likewise adept at securing the maximum publicity for the minimum expenditure. It was a railway full of ideas but short of money, so its publicity ventures were carefully thought out. It was one of the first companies to adopt a house style. The celebrated Gill Sans lettering was devised specifically for its publicity, and the lozenge-shaped 'LNER' was a predecessor of the company logo of modern times. Its posters employed well-known artists, often of modern, though not too modern, technique. Although most of its trains were drab and not very fast, it lavished much effort on publicizing a few good trains like the 'Flying Scotsman.' Here again the publicity was backed by real substance, for the Company was willing to spend money on building new advanced rolling stock for its handful of celebrated trains. Not only the 'Flying Scotsman' but also the 'Hook Continental' benefited from this, and the climax was the very striking trains designed for the streamlined 'Silver Jubilee,' 'West Riding Limited,' and 'Coronation.'

The LMS started badly, but in the end did well. In the 1920s its trains were not good, with average speeds lower than before the Great War. It was unwilling to spend money building distinctive new trains for particular services and its public image was deservedly poor. But it produced good posters. Norman Wilkinson, the best-known landscape and marine artist, served as its adviser, and dozens of Royal Academicians were commissioned to paint posters. In the 1930s the LMS pulled itself together and was ready to advertise the fact in a series of booklets and brochures. *The Track of the Royal Scot* was an instant success. *Travel LMS – The Best Way* was much more obviously sales literature but has lasting interest because, although published in 1935, its cover sports not one of Stanier's new locomotives, but an older Lancashire & Yorkshire type; presumably the publicity department still felt that locomotive policy was a minefield for the unwary. The annual *Holidays by LMS*, a thick illustrated guidebook with guesthouse listings, was designed

Left: *The GWR advertises some less well-known resorts in South Wales.*

Above: *The Great Central Railway flattered its directors by using their names for locomotives.*

Below: *The GWR's annual* Holiday Haunts.

Right: *An SR 'Battle of Britain' class nameplate.*

Center right: *A poster issued in the early years of British Railways.*

Bottom right: *Another LNER poster, showing the lozenge-shaped logo which that company used for some years.*

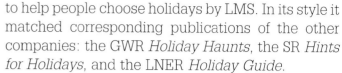

"THE FLYING SCOTSMAN", DRAWN BY "SILVER LINK", PICKING UP WATER AT SPEED

DINE WELL by LNER

1938

200 Restaurant Cars

to help people choose holidays by LMS. In its style it matched corresponding publications of the other companies: the GWR *Holiday Haunts*, the SR *Hints for Holidays*, and the LNER *Holiday Guide*.

One LMS innovation was its own film unit, the forerunner of British Transport Films that won so many prizes in the 1950s. Railways had in fact appeared in many films, right from the silent era. They were a frequent background for thrillers, lending themselves to dramatic scenes, atmospheric shots, and suspense. ('A Kiss in the Tunnel,' a short and daring film of 1900, showed other possibilities). The film as publicity had not been entirely ignored by the pre-grouping railways. The LNWR, for example, produced films of various holiday trips that the Company could offer.

With the talkies, steam locomotives could be exploited for their sound effects, and they were used in several feature films. *The Flying Scotsman*, a mediocre love drama of 1930 which included a glorious footplate fight between driver and fireman, was remarkable because, with sound equipment becoming available while it was being made, its first part was silent and its last part was with sound. There were other film dramas that showed railways, and a common feature of them all were trains whose locomotives would mysteriously change from shot to shot. An exception to this rule was *The Wrecker*, filmed on the SR, and whose climax was a destructive collision of locomotive and tractor; for this the SR could only sacrifice one old SECR 4-4-0, due for scrapping in any case. More memorable are the railway comedies. *Oh! Mr Porter*, set in Ireland but filmed on an SR branch line, was immensely popular and was a worthy predecessor of the postwar comedy, *The Titfield Thunderbolt*. These films have in common the portrayal of railways as small-scale, very local, very quaint, and inherently comic.

The LMS film unit had its origins in the popular success won by film of the 'Royal Scot' train's visit to North America, a film which was shown throughout Britain. Among subsequent films was *Coronation Scot*, a classic not only for its railway interest but for its advanced technique.

The best-known LMS railway film, however, was made by the GPO Film Unit in 1936. This was *Night Mail*, with production (John Grierson), music (Benjamin Britten) and poetry (W.H. Auden) by men who would become more famous and less impecunious in later years. Auden's words, covering the scenes as the mail train makes its nocturnal way into Scotland, still well-known, still reproduced in anthologies, go right to the heart of the railway age:
This is the night mail crossing the border,
Bringing the cheque and the postal order . . .
In the farm she passes no one wakes,
But a jug in a bedroom gently shakes.

Although freight was the most important business on most British railways, and used a much greater variety of vehicles, passenger vehicles (or coaching stock, as they were called) attracted greater interest. This was partly because the public had first-hand experience of coach design; it was ready to make comparisons, which was quite important in a competitive situation where, on many routes, passengers could choose between two or more railways. It was also partly because the design of a railway coach required ever-varying compromises between commerce and engineering, while its construction involved a high degree of craftsmanship that at its upper levels merged into industrial art. For the passenger and onlooker, the paintwork and the furnishings and the convenience of the vehicle were the main points of interest, while for the designer the essential problem was to reconcile the commercial need to carry as many passengers per ton of vehicle as possible with the demand for more comfort.

Previous pages: *A superior GNR train poses for the camera in 1900. It consists of five 12-wheel clerestory-roofed passenger vehicles and an eight-wheel van, hauled by one of the new Great Northern 4-4-2, or Atlantic, locomotives.*

Below: Sugar beet is loaded into 12-ton open cars at an LMS goods yard in 1934.

But with rising incomes people were able to pay for comfort, so it was natural that over the decades cost considerations took second place to customer satisfaction. Trains provided somewhat more comfort and speed than was strictly necessary, and hence fares were a little higher than they might have been, but that is what the public seemed to want. The number of passengers carried per ton of train fell, and with accelerating speeds this meant that horsepower per passenger grew even faster. The process of offering passengers more comfortable trains was, more often than not, affected by the competitive situation. For example, the other railways' imitation of the Midland Railway's decision to upgrade third class to second class standards was not immediate, but was inevitable. On the other hand, competition did not always work to the public's benefit. In Kent, where the competition between the two main railways bordered on the inane, the rival companies tended to fight their competitive battle with one or two ostentatiously excellent trains while neglecting the standards of their ordinary services.

Perhaps it was not so much the competitive situation, but the class situation, that determined the advance of passenger facilities. At the top of the social tree was royalty, and the provision of royal coaches and royal trains gave designers a chance to excel themselves and to try out all kinds of expensive novelties. In course of time these royal features filtered down to the first-class vehicles and eventually to the second and third, although this downward percolation might take several decades. In the case of sleeping cars, the initiative started with the first class; the London & Birmingham Railway had seats convertible to berths in its 'bed carriages' of the 1840s, but it was not until the 1920s that the railway companies began to provide sleeping accommodation for third-class passengers. The fitting of flexible gangways between coaches was a

Left: GWR clerestory-roofed rolling stock is used to deliver spectators to a 1908 football match. Special trains at weekends probably paid their way despite the low fares, because they utilized vehicles that would otherwise be idle.

further apart, so the passenger had more leg room, and the seats were padded. First class was opulent, with thick soft upholstery and quilted wall coverings absorbing much of the jolting and noise associated with rail travel.

The second half of the nineteenth century witnessed an advance that was to bring the better rail vehicles to a level not far removed from the average coach of the mid-twentieth century. The improvements took the form of smoother riding and better lighting, sanitation, ventilation, and heating, as well as the provision of new services like dining and sleeping cars. There was also an improvement in safety gained by better brakes and the greater inherent strength of railway vehicles as they grew in size and weight.

Better riding, despite higher speeds, was obtained partly from improved track but also from innovations in the mechanical design of vehicles. Suspension still relied on leaf springs, and improvements here were marginal, but the gradual introduction of coaches riding on bogies, four- or six-wheel trucks that had freedom to swivel, made all the difference. The earliest railway coaches had run on two rigid axles, like a goods wagon or road coach. Six-wheel coaches had an equally rigid chassis, which apart from accentuating up-and-down motion as the vehicle passed over rail joints, also produced a shock when the vehicle hit a curve. With a bogie, these horizontal and vertical oscillations were moderated, although that was not the main reason for their introduction.

They were introduced because there were good economic reasons for making coaches longer, and vehicles with rigid axles were restricted to a wheelbase short enough for them to negotiate curves without bumping and grinding. However, many engineers continued to build four- and six-wheelers. It was not until 1923 that the construction of such short vehicles ceased, the last proponent being the Caledonian Railway, which preferred them for some of its Edinburgh suburban services. The GWR, like several other companies, built bogie coaches for its best long-distance services but for years continued to build short vehicles for local trains. Francis Webb of the LNWR, who was slow to approve of any innovation of which he did not hold the patent, tried to obtain the same advantages by designing coaches that had two sets of four wheels, the inner pair of each set being rigidly attached and the outer pair having some sideplay. These LNWR coaches at 42 feet were not much longer than ordinary six-wheelers, whereas the true bogie vehicles were already 50 feet or more. In the 1870s, influenced by American practice, the Midland Railway introduced some 12-wheel vehicles, using three-axle bogies, and this innovation was copied to a limited extent by other

FIRST CLASS.

SECOND CLASS.

THIRD CLASS.
ENGLAND IN 1842: GOING TO THE DERBY.
DRAWN BY JOHN LEECH.

Above: *Passenger class distinction in 1842. By the end of the century third class travel had been unrecognizibly transformed.*

somewhat faster process; first introduced on a royal train for Queen Victoria in 1869, it had spread to several other trains by 1900.

After about 1850 the railway coach began to shed many of the road coach features that it had inherited. However, the basic unit was still the compartment, a relic of the days when a railway coach was little more than three road-coach bodies placed end-to-end on a railway underframe. There were three classes of travel, marked by varying size and opulence of compartments. At mid-century the third class passenger could expect bare boards for seats, and partitions that did not reach the ceiling. In the second class the partitions were full height and

LIVERPOOL EXPERIENCE MANCHESTER
RAILWAY — COMPANY

A CARRIAGE OF THE FIRST CLASS.
L. & M. R'Y. 1838.

THIRD

Above left: *A first class vehicle of the 1830s.*

Far left: *Queen Victoria's LNWR saloon, used by the Queen in the 1890s.*

Left: *A Midland Railway third-class six-wheeler.*

Top right: *An LNWR observation car of 1913, built for North Wales.*

Center right: *An SR coach, showing the Pullman-style gangway.*

Bottom right: *A third-class non-corridor coach, as used for SR suburban services.*

companies. The tare weight of the vehicles was increased, but riding was smoother, and the idea was therefore most useful for dining and sleeping cars.

In the last quarter of the nineteenth century the MR was the pace-setter in passenger facilities. It imported various types of Pullman car, which for some reason did not win great public acclaim; either the British resented paying the required supplementary fare, or they were satisfied with what they already had, but they certainly did not clamor for an extension of Pullman services. Later, some railways, especially in the south, did introduce Pullman trains for the more prosperous commuters or holidaymakers, but they never really caught on in Britain. However, some of the engineering features of the Pullman cars, including their three-axle bogies, made a lasting impression, as did the provision of good toilets, heating and enhanced lighting.

Much more influential was the MR's decision to abolish the austere third-class standard of accommodation. It did this by withdrawing third-class and relabelling the old second-class as third. Second-class as a classification, and third-class as a standard, were thereby ended, and other companies at their own speed followed suit, mainly in the 1890s, although the LNWR refused to change its ways until 1912, and the Great North of Scotland had never offered second-class. By the mid-1920s the second-class designation was restricted to boat trains connecting with three-class continental railways, and some LNER suburban services.

By making third-class more comfortable and allowing third-class passengers to use the best and fastest trains, the MR did itself as well as railway travelers a great service. It opened up a mass market, for hitherto the third-class passenger had embarked unwillingly on a train, out of necessity rather than for pleasure. On the MR, and soon on other lines, third-class travel became something that it was possible to enjoy. Third-class fares remained low, but the sheer volume of extra passengers enhanced the MR's passenger revenue.

In the 1870s and 1880s sleeping and dining cars appeared on a number of railways for the benefit of first-class passengers. Bed carriages, in which seats could be re-arranged to permit a recumbent position, had been tried sporadically on several railways but the true sleeper, with permanent beds, was probably a six-wheeler introduced by the North British Railway in 1873 for Anglo-Scottish service on the East Coast route (it was imitated within weeks by the West Coast route). It had two large compartments with beds arranged longitudinally. Transverse beds would have been better, but there was not enough space to provide a six foot berth and a side corridor as well. The then broad-gauge GWR did not have this problem and in the 1880s introduced the arrangement of transverse beds and side corridor which later, with wider rolling stock, would become the standard for other railways.

Most of the sleeping car designs included toilets, and this feature spread in the 1880s to other vehicles, almost always first-class. At first, the toilets were shared between two adjacent compartments, but in 1882 the Great Northern Railway introduced coaches with side corridors, giving all compartments access to toilets at each end of the vehicle. This facility was slowly extended to third-class passengers. Separate provision was made for ladies and

Left: The novelty of the Midland Railway's Pullman sleepers attracted much comment, both admiring and sceptical. This selection of views published in 1874 seems to reflect several attitudes.

THE RAILWAY QUESTION — NOTES IN A PULLMAN PALACE CAR ON THE MIDLAND RAILWAY

Top left: *Interwar dining car decor on the LNER.*

Top right: *A first-class sleeping compartment as offered by the MR around 1910.*

Above: *Lancashire & Yorkshire Railway suburban stock of 1920.*

gentlemen, this being an instance when Victorian manners achieved a social benefit that was denied later generations, for it was not long before gender differentiation of toilets was abandoned. Another case of declining standards was smoking accommodation. In the early decades of railways, smoking was customarily forbidden on the trains, the railways being especially concerned about the first class; they said the upholstery retained the smell, but probably were more concerned about the upholstery getting scorched. Addicts had to steal a hasty drag whenever the train stopped at a station. Later, most railways provided a compartment for smokers, and in 1868 Parliament was persuaded by the reforming MP John Stuart Mill to require all but the

shortest trains to include a smoking coach. As the years passed, smoking accommodation increased until it exceeded nonsmoking, and by the 1940s nonsmoking compartments were very much a minority. Moreover, should a passenger light up in a nonsmoker there was no certainty that railway staff (or, in at least one instance, the courts) would enforce the no smoking rule.

The Great Northern was the pioneer in the provision of dining cars, for it introduced a Pullman diner between London and Leeds in 1879. Other lines followed suit, although the West Coast route did not provide dining cars until 1891, the LNWR believing that passengers preferred the Preston meal stop. Initially, it was only first-class passengers who benefited. Other classes brought their own food, or purchased one of the quite sumptuous lunch baskets on sale at stations, or joined the rush at a meal stop, where trains would halt long enough for passengers to consume a meal that was allegedly either too hot or too cold. In the absence of gangways between vehicles, passengers would go to the dining car at a station, or would sit in it for the whole trip. Occupying a dining seat for the entire journey enabled the passenger to while away long journeys by eating several meals. The Midland Railway was among those prepared to make advance seat reservations in the dining car, and its post-grouping successor the LMS carried on this practice.

Although it was the first decade of the twentieth century that witnessed the large-scale provision of passenger amenities that had hitherto been limited to first-class passengers or to a few very select trains, the closing years of the previous century saw the introduction of perhaps the most important amenity of all: trains that had adequate brakes. By the 1880s, handbrakes operated by train staff positioned down the train were being replaced by powered brakes using compressed air or vacuum, but such brakes were not automatic. If a train broke, the loose end would not stop, a serious matter if the train was climbing a gradient, as the horrific Armagh accident of 1889 demonstrated. It required an Act of Parliament to force all railways to introduce automatic brakes for their passenger trains, and even then there was a long debate about which type to use. In the end, to their ultimate cost, the railways could not agree and they split into two camps, those using the vacuum and those using the compressed air brake. Anglo-Scottish services on the East Coast route had to use coaches with both kinds of brake.

The automatic brake made it easier to devise a good passenger alarm system. This took the form of the communication cord which, when pulled by a passenger, opened a valve connecting with the brake system and caused a brake application. The guard then merely had to go down the train to dis-

cover in which compartment the alarm chain had been pulled. Previous systems had included a cord, which could be pulled by the guard or by a passenger, that caused bells to ring both on the locomotive and in the guard's van.

By the turn of the century the side corridor, and the gangway between vehicles, had become accepted as a concept, although they were still rare in practice. Their advantages were clear, although their costs were also evident. Of all the innovations that struck at the goal of carrying the maximum

number of passengers per ton of train, the side corridor was the most damaging, for it reduced by 20 percent the carrying capacity of a vehicle. Compartments in non-corridor stock could seat five passengers abreast (the broad-gauge GWR had managed eight abreast at one time). With a side corridor, passengers could sit only four per side, and then with little freedom of movement. But the corridor made access to a toilet easy and, once the flexible gangway between vehicles became practical, was of unquestioned utility. It enabled train staff to

Above left: *An LMS coach bogie, with some older 12-wheeled vehicles in the background.*

Above: *Interior of an LMS corridor coach.*

Left: *The articulated suspension of the 'Silver Jubilee' train.*

Right: *One of the earlier LMS coaches.*

Above: *An LNER buffet car, designed by Gresley.*

reach all parts of the train (an area of potential staff cuts), and it enabled all passengers to reach the dining car in a flow that could conform to speed of meal service. The through-put of the dining car was thereby increased and it was not long before dining facilities were extended to third-class passengers. These advantages were denied to passengers in Kent, for the South Eastern & Chatham right at the end of its life still possessed only a handful of corridor vehicles, mainly for its boat trains.

The GWR, in the 1890s, introduced all-corridor trains with gangway connections. At first, these gangways were not placed centrally at the coachends, but at the side so as to form a continuous passage in line with the side corridors. But this caused complications as it meant that a coach could be the wrong way round, with its gangways not mating with its neighbors. It was not long however, therefore, before the central gangway became standard. However, non-standardization (which was almost a British railways tradition) survived in the coexistence of two different designs of gangway. A few railways preferred the Pullman type. This was quite wide, and rested on the American-style automatic coupler; adjacent gangways were not attached to each other but were brought together by the coupler, which held the coaches closer than did the normal British screw coupling. The other gangway, British-style, was longer and was of bellows construction, with adjacent gangways held together by clamps. Apart from Pullman cars, coaches of the Great Northern Railway and those used in the East coast Anglo-Scottish service employed the Pullman system, but for many decades the British gangway predominated. Pullman-style ends had to carry buffers even though they did not need them, their buckeye couplings serving that function. But they carried buffers, as well as screw couplings, simply so that they could be coupled to non-Pullman-style vehicles and, moreover, their own couplings had to be folded away to allow this. The merits of the two gangways were disputed, but certainly in derailments the automatic buckeye coupler was superior because it tended to hold the coaches together. The Pullman type was not standardized until the 1950s.

A long-needed innovation was introduced by the GWR at the turn of the century. This was central heating, achieved by under-seat radiators fed by a steam line from the locomotive. Hitherto, passengers had needed to swathe themselves in traveling rugs during winter journeys, just as in the days of the stage coach. The railways did provide footwarmers, but these were only a palliative. Coach illumination was also improving, linked with the design of coach roofs. The clerestory roof, in which the central section was raised and pierced with side windows, enhanced daytime illumination and provided space for night lamps, but it was more expensive to build and needed extra man-hours to keep clean. Many railways still preferred it in the early years of the twentieth century, but it was soon replaced by the elliptical roof. The latter, unlike the arc roof that had hitherto been the alternative shape, rose quite high and provided extra space for baggage. Previously, coaches were rather lower than the maximum allowable height. Different railways preferred different roof profiles, but it became the practice to build coaches as high as possible, and the clerestory lost favor. Some coaches had a pronounced bulbous form, and on the LBSCR such vehicles were nicknamed 'balloon stock.' The better trains tended to be composed of homogeneous stock, although the LNWR was notorious for combining in one train coaches of varying shapes and sizes.

Oil lamps long survived, but by 1875 gas lamps were preferred, although the stored gas was a danger in accidents. The LNWR, never able to resist a promising economy, at one point believed it had solved the lighting problem by eliminating lamps and painting the compartment ceilings with luminous paint. However, it later redeemed itself by a wholesale adoption of electric lighting, its principal trains being so fitted by the 1890s, only seven years after the LBSCR had first shown that it was practical to drive a dynamo from a coach axle.

Together with the extension of new comforts to more trains and to cheaper-class passengers, the last years of peace before 1914 saw the steady replacement of timber frames by steel. Many companies resisted this change, but those which used coaches over 55 feet long found that timber, despite its cheapness and convenience, was impracticable for the main frames at least. For the most part, coach bodies continued to be of timber, although there were a few examples of steel outer panels.

Some railways began to build wider coaches. For the formerly broad-gauge GWR this was easy, and its 'Dreadnought' coaches were 9 feet 5 inches wide and 70 feet long. But even the GWR had to recess the end doors so as to reduce the overhang on curved track. Other companies found that by removing a few lineside structures they could operate 9 feet-

wide coaches, although the SECR, whose lines had been built as cheaply as possible, could not do this. Every inch counted. Often, to gain an inch or two, door handles were recessed into the body of the coach. A width of 9 feet was especially valuable for suburban stock, because it just enabled six-a-side seating, bringing coach capacity, typically, to 60 seats. The GER was one of the pioneers of this trend, and was so pleased with its success that it withdrew its 8 feet-wide coaches, split them down the middle, inserted new central sections, and returned them to traffic as 9-footers. Later, when companies began to replace their close-coupled four-wheel suburban coaches with bogie coaches, the GER achieved a similar cheap transformation by mounting pairs of its four-wheeler bodies on new bogie underframes. Serving a region that was not especially prosperous, the GER understood the difficulties of making ends meet, and it was quite appropriate that in the 1890s, it became the first railway to provide dining facilities for third-class passengers. Here, too, it economized, for instead of using bogie vehicles for its dining cars it chose to put together a dining-car set of three six-wheelers linked to each other (but not with the rest of the train) by gangways.

Nigel Gresley of the Great Northern succeeded

in reducing the key ton-per-seat statistic of sub-urban vehicles by making a success of the articulated trainset. In this, adjoining coach-ends shared a single bogie, and Gresley's first articulated trains consisted of four two-car sets coupled together, each set riding on just three bogies. Gresley also built dining car sets on the same principle, and used it for the streamlined trains he later built for the LNER.

The GNR and its successor the LNER also made a practice of designing new trains for specific services. This began with Gresley's four-coach sets for the London-Sheffield service, and culminated with the 'Silver Jubilee' and 'Coronation' of the 1930s. The LNWR, long a specialist in higgledy-piggledy formations, mended its ways to the extent of producing expensive trains with impressive rolling stock, first for the Liverpool transatlantic boat trains, and then for the afternoon 'Corridor' service between London and Glasgow, although in the latter case it could not resist spoiling the picture by including old-style clerestory dining cars among the new elliptical roofed stock.

After the railway grouping the number of different designs slowly declined. More immediate was the disappearance of the old company liveries. The paintwork of passenger stock had been one of the glories of the railway scene, with some companies lavishing ten or more coats of paint and varnish on a vehicle so as to guarantee the required finish. Most vehicles had a luxurious display of gilt lettering on top of their basic livery. With over a hundred railways in existence before the grouping, this meant a profuse variety of colors. Different shades of maroon were selected by the NER and SECR, but the MR's crimson lake put these two very much in the shade. The West Coast partners, LNWR and Caledonian, chose spilt milk for the upper panels and plum for the lower (Caldeonian plum being reddish and LNWR plum purplish). Quite unusual was the LSWR's salmon-pink uppers and brown lower panels, although towards the end of its life the LSWR moved to a cheaper brunswick green. The GWR had likewise found its chocolate and cream livery rather expensive, had changed to an unexciting maroon, but then after World War One returned to the glories of the old colors. The GNR

Top: *A stopping train at Redhill, hauled by an SECR 0-4-4 tank locomotive. The train is of 'birdcage' stock, so called because of the guard's glass-paned lookout position above the roof.*

Left: *Flat-sided stock, designed by the SR for lines with narrow clearances, forms a stopping train from Brighton in BR days.*

varnished teak survived the grouping, being chosen as the LNER livery, but was not so agreeable when steel-paneled stock appeared and was finished with teak-color paint. The LBSCR varnished mahogany was another scheme that favored the exposure of the natural wood, and was cheaper than conventional multi-coat painting. The new LMS adopted a maroon version of the MR's red, while the Southern chose green, changing from olive to malachite green in the 1930s.

The placing of doors, and the choice between compartmented and open interiors, were the two main themes around which coach designs evolved in the interwar years. It had long been the practice to provide each compartment with a door at both sides, even when a corridor gave access to doors at the ends of the vehicle. Public preference was said to be the basis for this pattern, for all other considerations (apart from speed of loading, which was unimportant on long-distance trains but vital on suburban) favored end doors. Wherever there was a door there was a draught, so eliminating doors leading to the outside air would have been a great advantage. Moreover, each door represented extra money, both in capital investment and in maintenance. But although some companies experimented with the elimination of certain doors on corridor stock, it was not until after the railway grouping that this became standard practice for long-distance rolling stock. Suburban trains continued to be non-corridor, while other stopping trains habitually used older coaches handed down from long-distance services. All four companies, as they reduced the number of doors on corridor stock, began to take advantage of the situation to install deeper, wider, windows. These had upper sliding

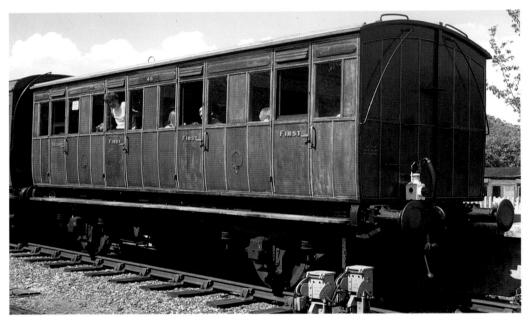

Top: *A GWR corridor coach of the 1930s, with the deep window and sliding toplights that were then in favor.*

Above: *One of the last four-wheeled coaches, used by the North London Railway for suburban work.*

Left: *GWR trains at Moor Street Station, Birmingham. The long, wide, passenger vehicle was designed with inset doors in order to fit available clearances.*

Right: *The 'Devon Belle' of the Southern Railway.*

Below: *A publicity photograph showing the interior of the 'Devon Belle' observation car.*

ventilators, thereby eliminating the downward-sliding windows that were traditionally installed in the doors, adjusted with a leather strap whose holes could be slipped over a brass peg in the door. Such windows were retained in the doors that were kept and were a necessity when door handles were on the outside of the train only. But these windows quite often jammed in the closed position, and pas-

sengers needed help to open the door; this was one of the main cares of station porters, ears cocked to catch the sound of frantic tapping on the glass windows. Even with door releases that could be opened from the inside there could be mishaps, because in designing catches that were child-proof no provision could be made for adults who did not have powerful fingers.

Most coaches continued to be compartmented, but the open layout became popular on the LMS, and to a lesser extent on the LNER. This saloon layout was not entirely new, because it had been used for dining cars and also for certain vehicles in the previous century, notably in the 'family saloons' that could be occupied for the price of a supplementary fare by an entire family. The LMS continued to use wood for many of its designs, although it also acquired some all-steel coaches. The latter weighed about three tons, or 11 percent, more than comparable vehicles with wooden frames and side panels, which was one reason why the move to steel construction was long delayed. It was not until the price of timber rose relative to steel that the British railways finally abandoned timber.

Whereas on the GWR coach design merely developed on lines already laid down, the new Southern Railway. faced with a variety of traditions and practices brought by its constituent companies, found it necessary to introduce new standard de-

Below: *A publicity photograph showing the interior of the 'Devon Belle' observation car.*

Above: *A train of fish vans on the Lancashire & Yorkshire Railway in 1913.*

Left: *Farm traffic on the LMS in the 1930s. Livestock movement required careful planning and much labor, with attendants occasionally traveling on the train.*

signs right at the start. They were usually 58 feet long, but they came in three widths because the Kentish main line could only accept 8 foot 6 inches, and the Hastings line was limited to 8 feet. The SR stayed with timber frames and steel side panels, but decided to standardize the Pullman gangway and the associated buckeye coupler, both of which were already in use on the Pullman trains it had inherited. It also built some saloon coaches with spacious interiors that could be labeled, according to need, as first or third class, or even second class for the boat trains.

The LNER continued under Gresley with Great Northern designs and concepts. More articulated suburban sets were built, and special trains were constructed to provide the 'Flying Scotsman' service. The GWR also built special trainsets for its 'Cornish Riviera Limited,' but the LMS, even for its 'Royal Scot' and 'Coronation Scot,' merely used standard vehicles which, in the latter case, were given a distinctive livery. The LMS, outshone by the LNER in this respect, finally changed its mind in 1939 and built special vehicles for the 'Coronation Scot,' but the war intervened and the vehicles were

never used in that service.

The peak of LNER, and indeed British, design came with the trains specially designed for the 'Coronation' and 'West Riding Limited.' The 'Coronation' was a nine-coach formation weighing only 312 tons, thanks to the use of articulated trainsets which saved the weight of four bogies. Its last vehicle was an observation car, quite rare in British practice, whose end had a beavertail configuration to match the wedge-shaped front end of the streamlined locomotive. The outside finish was enamelled, with light blue for the upper panels and dark blue for the lower. The interiors were open, but clever design enabled the first-class seats to occupy alcoves, each chair swiveling from window to table. The decor was modern, made great use of aluminum, but was not obtrusive. All in all, this train was a fine example of contemporary industrial art, and passengers willingly paid the supplementary fare that was levied for its use.

Postwar designs built by the companies in the couple of years before nationalization introduced new door permutations. The GWR, while staying with end doors, added one or two doors on both

Left: *An LNER vehicle designed for heavy loads.*

Below: *A GWR freight train at Cardiff, hauled by one of the 0-6-2 tank engines specially designed for the winding Welsh valleys.*

sides. The LNER showed a novel approach by building vehicles with doors not at the ends but part-way down the sides, thereby reducing the maximum distance a passenger might need to walk in order to reach a seat. The SR built 65 feet coaches with end doors, and began to favor open layouts; some of its vehicles provided compartments as well as an open saloon section.

With nationalization there came another change of color as British Railways introduced its own color scheme. After some experimentation, maroon and cream were chosen for long distance stock, with maroon for other services. But the SR green continued for Southern Electric, and for a period the Western Region painted a few of its best trains the old chocolate and cream. Meanwhile, arriving just in time to enter the steam era, standard BR coach designs were introduced. These tended to follow LMS practice, although all-steel construction became the rule. The bogies were not entirely satisfactory, because they were very sensitive to poor or delayed maintenance, and BR began a hunt for a more satisfactory design. At the close of the steam era it was possible to see trains made up of vehicles riding on three different designs of bogie.

In contrast to coaching stock, the British railway freightcar stock lagged behind other countries in its technical development, and when the steam age came to an end in the 1960s it was an anachronism, typically being of small capacity, manually braked, and with loose hook-and-link couplings. Although iron frames had been tried in the 1860s, and the GWR went over to metal frames in 1879, companies long persisted with wooden frames on the grounds first of expense and second of the ease with which wooden frames could be repaired at even the smallest freightcar depot. Freightcar bodies for the most part remained of wood, with metal strengtheners.

Axleboxes originally contained grease, which tended to be stiff when cold. Gradually oil was substituted in the nineteenth century, but its increased fluidity meant that freightcars left on sidings were liable to be set in motion by the wind. This was an

Right: *A private-owner 12-ton coal wagon.*

additional stimulus to the provision of proper brakes. Traditionally, freight trains were halted by the locomotive brakes and by the brakevan, which was the guard's van at the end of the train with a manual brake.

The brakes that were fitted to freightcars were also manual, operated by a long lever that could be pinned down by brakesmen when the train was halted for that purpose on the brink of a steep gradient. This technique of braking, a combination of locomotive, brakevan, and wagon brakes, was archaic even at the beginning of the twentieth century. Another archaic feature was the loose coupling. The 3-link chain was easy to handle in freightyards, where train assembly could be carried out by shunters deftly swinging the coupling chains on and off the hooks with their shunting poles, but it caused a good deal of crashing and banging as the buffers of adjacent freightcars crashed into or drew away from each other in accordance with the gradients, the pull of the engine and the operation of the brakes.

When competition, and a desire to improve matters, caused the railways to seek ways of running express freight trains, specially equipped vehicles were used. These had continuous brakes, which could be controled from the engine, and were close-coupled with screw couplings. Such freightcars were more expensive, and to save money many were not provided with continuous brakes but were simply 'piped.' That is, they carried the brake-pipe so that they could be marshaled in a continuously braked train. Freight trains were classified according to their speeds. At the lower end of the scale were the slow, drag, freights with no continuous brake. Then, there were trains that were allowed to move a little faster, consisting mainly of vehicles with manual lever brakes but with a handful of continuous-brake cars next to the engine. At the top of the scale were 'fully fitted' trains, entirely equipped with the continuous brake, which could run at passenger train speeds. Even faster delivery could be obtained by sending freight by passenger train. Some perishables traffic, like fish and newspapers, ran in vehicles that were of coaching standard and could be attached to the rear of passenger trains.

Open cars, sometimes with a frame for supporting a tarpaulin, were the most common type of freightcar. Covered vehicles, or vans, were also numerous and were in demand for commodities that might easily be damaged by rain or locomotive sparks. As the decades passed, specialized vehicles for carrying commodities like oil, milk, and fruit appeared. With specialized stock, the virtual impossibility of finding a return load partly offset the advantage of having a car designed for the precise job.

Coal was the most important freight, but the railways possessed very few mineral cars to carry it,

although they did operate their own 'Loco' vehicles to supply their locomotive depots with coal. Most coal and much other traffic was carried in 'private-owner' vehicles. These were owned by the user, who registered the cars with the local railway and had the right to send them, at a price, to any destination. The railway companies undertook to move these vehicles, but the owners were responsible for their maintenance. This arrangement had the advantage that it saved the railways considerable capital investment, but it had disadvantages as well. Private owners were reluctant to make any changes in their operations. Their wagons had to be returned immediately and could not carry a return load. Moreover, the owners often failed to maintain their vehicles in good order, and breakdowns en route could be costly and disruptive for the railway companies. In the 1880s the Midland Railway thought it had found a solution to this problem. It purchased the vehicles belonging to collieries on its lines, but the

Left: *LNER freight rolling stock on exhibition. The heavy-load vehicles are hauled by the LNER's only Garratt locomotive.*

only result was that it acquired a ramshackle collection of open cars while the colliery owners used the money to buy themselves a new fleet of coal wagons. It was while engaged in this ill-conceived buy-out that the Midland painted 'MR' in large letters on the sides of the vehicles in question, an idea that soon became general practice for all railway-owned freight cars.

Even in 1950 the preponderant mass of freight vehicles had capacities of only 10 to 12 tons, which was inefficient and raised costs. The companies had sporadically tried to introduce larger vehicles, but such attempts were usually frustrated by shippers, who did not want to alter their loading and unloading facilities to suit the railways. The companies were somewhat more successful with another endeavor, the introduction of containers that could be moved on railway flatcars but also on road vehicles for pick-up and delivery. These containers were quite small, too, but they succeeded in retaining for the railways much merchandise traffic that would otherwise have been lost to road transport operators with their attractive offer of 'door-to-door' transport.

Like so many other apparent novelties, containers had in fact been used earlier by British railways. In Edwardian times both the LNWR and L & Y railways carried some coal in boxes loaded on to flatcars. This coal was destined for ships' bunkers and was easier to handle when boxed. The LSWR was even more advanced with its 'piggyback' service for imported meat. This meat was loaded into horse-drawn road vans at Southampton, the vans were loaded on to LSWR flatcars and on arrival in London were attached to fresh horses for delivery to butchers and markets. A similar technique, using road tanker trailers, was later used by the GWR and SR for transporting milk from the West of England to London.

Above: *The very useful general-utility van of the SR, used typically for parcels. The fast freight on the left is hauled by one of Drummond's unsuccessful LSWR 4-6-0 passenger locomotives.*

Right: *A London-bound coal train on the Midland Railway's main line.*

Left: *A GWR 'Hall' in charge of a cattle train in BR days.*

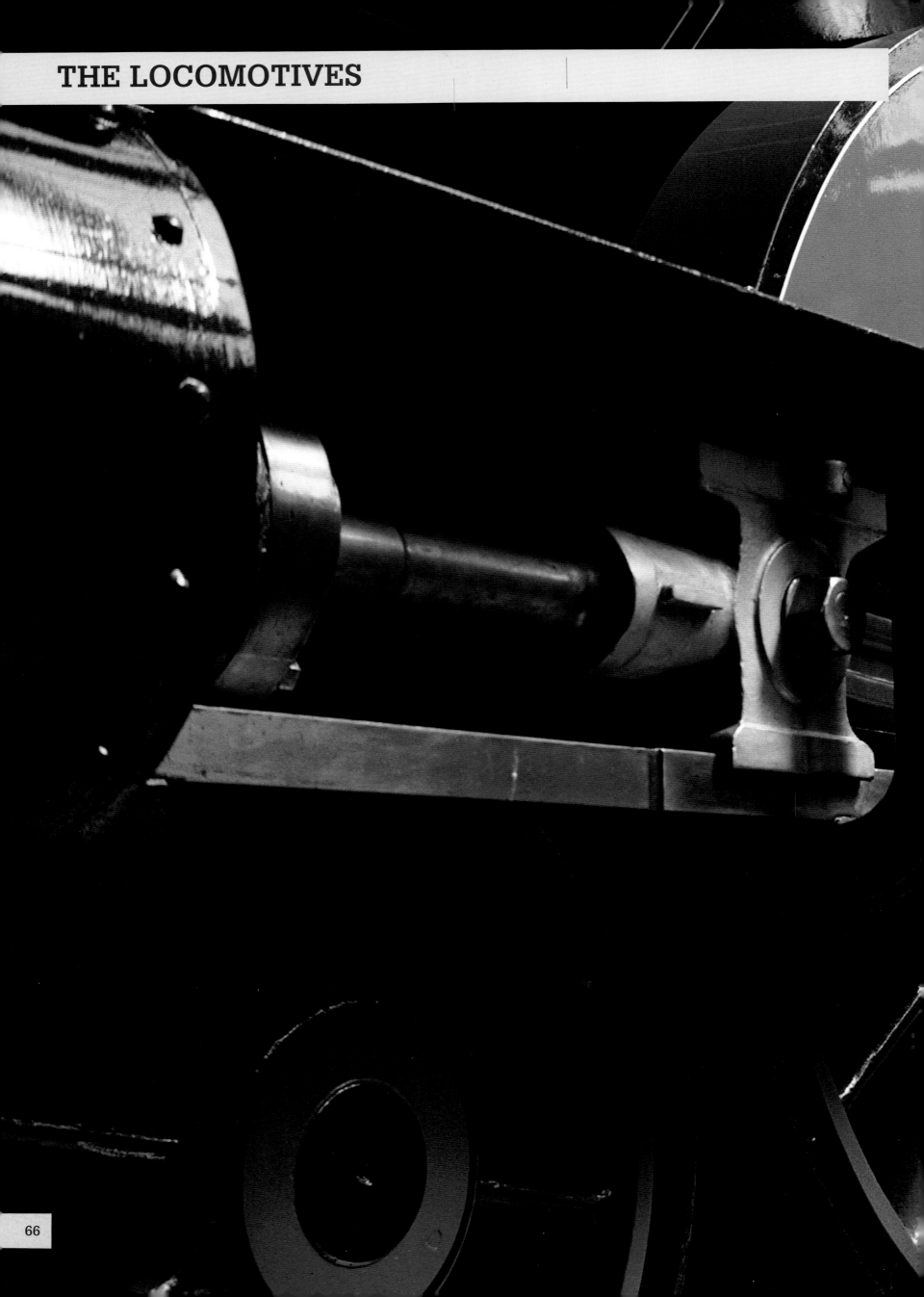

By the close of the nineteenth century the British railway companies had turned to the 4-4-0 wheel arrangement for their passenger trains, and remained with the 0-6-0 for freight. In fact, the 0-6-0 would remain in production until the 1940s, by which time the concept was already a century old. Two cylinders, located between the frames, were the standard for both 4-4-0 and 0-6-0 types, although there were occasional exceptions. In fact, inside cylinders, adopted because they apparently produced fewer oscillations, had several disadvantages, being cramped, inaccessible, and dependent on a cranked axle that was expensive to manufacture and maintain. But it was not until the late 1940s that outside cylinders with outside valve gear were finally triumphant. The 0-6-0 wheel arrangement was also far from perfect; the absence of a leading bogie meant that the wheels tended to swing and bang against the rails.

The persistence of old standards beyond the time when they should have been superseded was characteristic of British locomotive design, but it was only the reverse side of a much more favorable picture. Conservatism had its advantages. It minimized the premature acceptance of fashionable but half-baked ideas, and it gave techniques times to perfect themselves. Above all, therefore, it tended to produce locomotives that worked well and were reliable in traffic, which was what the operating staff most needed. At the same time, with long-tried features established as a basis, trials of innovations were likely to be more fruitful.

By the turn of the century inside frames had become standard. Outside frames, in which the driving wheels were enclosed and thus restrained in

Previous pages: *Outside cylinders and inside valve gear was a common arrangement for passenger locomotives like this fine Great Northern 4-4-2.*

Left: *A quite typical British inside-cylinder 0-6-0. This is one of a large class built by the Caledonian Railway.*

Right: *An 1895 design of outside-framed 4-4-0 built by the GWR. This is* Cornubia, *which survived into the 1950s.*

Below: *The celebrated 'Midland Compound,' as originally built.*

the unlikely event of becoming detached, had been superseded except on the GWR, which would build some outside-framed 4-4-0s as late as the 1930s (the GWR was a company that was ever reluctant to say goodbye to the past). Alongside the 4-4-0s and 0-6-0s worked other types. The 'Single,' an express locomotive with only one driving axle, was still favored on some railways, especially the Midland. The absence of heavy coupling rods made it a well-balanced design, and the invention of steam sanding of the rails gave it a fresh lease of life by moderating its greatest defect, wheel-slip. Another predecessor of the 4-4-0, the 2-4-0, was still strongly represented; on the LBSCR and LSWR it took the form of an 0-4-2.

Also, possible successors to the 4-4-0 and 0-6-0 were in sight. The 4-6-0, which would become a favorite wheel arrangement for passenger engines, had been introduced on the Highland Railway for freight work over its heavily graded main line. An enlarged 4-4-0, the 4-4-2, had also appeared in the hope of combining the excellence of the 4-4-0 with a bigger firebox and hence greater horsepower output. For heavy freight, an enlargement of the 0-6-0 resulted in the 0-8-0.

Whereas in the earlier decades of the railway age the transition to bigger locomotives had proceeded quite smoothly, however, the enlargement of existing types at the end of the century was less successful. Railways found that producing a larger version of the 4-4-0 in the form of a 4-6-0 or 4-4-2 ('Atlantic') could, unexpectedly, produce a sluggish or uneconomical machine. Dugald Drummond, the locomotive engineer who served two Scottish railways and then the LSWR, provided his employers with a

sturdy range of robust and capable 4-4-0s, but his LSWR 4-6-0s were failures. Evidently what had been good enough in the past was not going to be good enough for the future, and the trend towards more powerful locomotives demanded by heavier and faster trains would require new thinking. Quality, not size, was the key.

The first problem to be tackled was the poor utilization of steam. Much of it condensed into water before it had a chance to convert its pressure into tractive energy. At the same time, it left the cylinders retaining a good deal of pressure which was wasted by being sent direct to the chimney. A remedy for the first problem was to reheat the steam to a very high temperature before it entered the cylinders. The first practical superheater was devised in Germany, and was a supplementary bank of bent steamtubes in the smokebox, heated by firebox gases. It added to maintenance costs, as it was a vulnerable unit, and the superheated steam demanded new kinds of cylinder lubricants, but it was of great value for engines running hard over long periods (which is why it was not fitted to shunting locomotives). It was introduced slowly to Britain, but in many cases it revolutionized locomotive performance. Two classes of Atlantic locomotive, the L & Y inside-cylinder design and the Ivatt outside-cylinder type on the Great Northern, which had hitherto been merely satisfactory, suddenly became

Top left: Hardwicke, *a simple-expansion 2-4-0 of the LNWR.*

Left: *The 'Midland Compound' in its later form.*

Above center: *Large and small GWR mixed-traffic 4-6-0s, a 'Manor' on the left and a 'Hall' on the right.*

Above right: *An outside frame 4-4-0 design that the GWR produced as late as the 1930s and initially named in honor of earls.*

outstanding, so much so that the GN Atlantics were copied by the LBSCR. While the improvement was usually described in terms of how much coal and water was consumed per horsepower-hour, the real effect of superheating was that an engine of a given size could produce significantly more horsepower. Engineers never questioned the efficacy of super-heating, although they did differ on the ideal temperature to which the steam should be raised. The GWR, which had other ways of improving perform-ance, always preferred low-temperature superheat, as it produced fewer complications, but in the end this policy was shown to be mistaken.

Another line of approach was the compound locomotive, in which steam passed from one or more high-pressure cylinders to be re-used in one or more low-pressure cylinders. Several permutations of cylinders were used. In the late nineteenth century the LNWR persisted unsuccessfully for many years with the construction of compounds with one inside low-pressure and two outside high-pressure cylinders before, as a kind of gambler's last throw, changing to two high-pressure and two low-pres-sure cylinders. Of this collection of designs the most charitable judgment is that some were better than others. On the other hand, Walter Smith, chief draughtsman of the NER, cooperated with his friend S.W. Johnson, locomotive superintendent of the Midland Railway, to evolve a locomotive with two

low-pressure outside cylinders and one inside high-pressure cylinder. A locomotive with this layout was built for the NER, but the concept achieved its greatest success with the 'Midland Compound' 4-4-0. This design not only hauled the MR's best trains for the remainder of that company's life, but was also built by the MR's successor, the LMS, so that in the end almost 250 units were built. For their size, these engines had high haulage capacity and comparatively low fuel consumption.

It was claimed that compounding made super-heating unnecessary, but in fact a superheated compound locomotive was theoretically best of all, provided it was used for duties demanding a consistently high power output. Compound loco-motives were more expensive to build and maintain, however, and demanded more careful driving, so they never found lasting favor on British railways.

On the GWR a revolution in locomotive design was achieved in the first decade of the new century, which would have an important long-term effect on British locomotives. Borrowing some American and some French ideas, the locomotive superintendent George Churchward introduced a series of standard locomotives that resembled no other engines in the world. Their superficial appearance, which derived from their fundamental novelty, was quite astounding for a public that was habituated to locomotives with tall chimneys, round domes, and wheels half-concealed by deep splashers.

Above: *An LBSCR 4-4-2 Beachy Head, at work near Redhill.*

Top right: Twineham Court, *one of the GWR's original 2-cylinder 4-6-0 design, leaves Swansea with a cross-country train.*

Right: *The 'Midland Compound' design, as built by the LMS in the 1920s.*

Churchward preferred a tapered boiler, wider at the firebox end where most of the heat transfer took place. At the forward end it was supported by a saddle, and each half of this smokebox saddle was cast with one of the cylinders, a common American practice. It was possible to remove the cylinders without first moving the boiler. The boiler was domeless, the steam collector being placed instead in the highest part of the boiler. Safety valves were moved forward to the boiler center, and enclosed in what would become a GWR feature, the truncated, conical, concave-sided brass cover. A square (Belpaire) firebox was favored, rather like those used in continental Europe but with stronger, rounded, corners and wider water spaces. The cylinders were outside although, contrary to American practice, Churchward kept the valve gear inside the frames, where it was relatively inaccessible. But the main factors in the success of the Churchward locomotives were hidden. The new standard boilers included blast-

pipe and chimney proportions that were derived from theoretical calculations made in an American university and which other British designers did not take seriously. Secondly, Churchward was well aware of the energy loss caused by constricted steam passages. He used long-travel valves, which enabled the steam ports admitting and releasing steam to the cylinders to be very large. This meant that steam entry and exit was fast and unhampered. Drivers learned to open their regulators wide; the steam reached the cylinders with little loss of pressure, so it could be cut off at an early stage in each cycle, most of its work being done by expansion inside the cylinder.

The first of the Churchward range was a 4-6-0, which after some experimentation became the basis for the very fast and capable 'Saint' class. A somewhat similar freight 2-8-0 used many of the components, and further Churchward designs included 2-6-2 tank locomotives and a 2-6-0, the latter being

Above: Haughton Grange, *one of the intermediate GWR mixed-traffic 4-6-0 design, takes a train out of Snow Hill Station, Birmingham.*

Right: *One of Churchward's light 2-6-2 tank locomotives takes a stopping train out of Carmarthen.*

at the time an unusual wheel arrangement for Britain, although common in America; evidently Churchward realised the drawbacks of the 0-6-0, to which his 2-6-0 was a successor. After some experiments with imported French compound locomotives, Churchward concluded that locomotives incorporating his features could perform as well as compounds.

Towards the end of this innovative burst, Churchward designed some larger locomotives. First there came the four-cylinder 'Star' class, which was immediately successful and clearly outperformed all other British passenger locomotives. Then there was his one comparative failure, a 4-6-2 or 'Pacific,' of which only one example was built.

Right: An LNER 'V2' locomotive takes a Newcastle train from Carlisle.

Below: A GWR 'Star,' Princess Beatrice, on one of its last duties, hauling a Worcester-London train in 1949.

Bottom: A Caledonian Railway engineman with his highly-polished 4-4-0.

Finally, after World War One, came a fast freight 2-8-0 with a new, bigger boiler. Apart from the Pacific all the Churchward designs remained in service until the 1950s or beyond, often still performing the same duties for which they had been designed.

Progress on other railways was less spectacular. In Scotland the Drummond tradition still dominated, with the rival North British and Caledonian railways relying on very similar, sturdy, designs of 4-4-0 and 0-6-0, although for suburban tank engines the CR preferred the 0-4-4 wheel arrangement and the NBR the 4-4-2. Towards the end of its life the NBR, having found that its 4-4-0s were falling behind requirements, built some handsome 4-4-2 machines whereas the CR, when greater power became necessary for its heavily graded main line between Carlisle and Glasgow, chose the 4-6-0. The 4-6-0 was also the final choice of the Highland Railway, with its 'Clan' and 'Clan Goods' classes, which were virtually identical apart form their driving wheel size.

The North Eastern Railway was also following this path, although in the final years its 4-4-2 type developed into a 4-6-2. Being a coal-hauler, it had a large stock of 0-6-0 locomotives, but also introduced the 0-8-0 so that it could increase line capacity and reduce costs by operating heavier trains. Its neighbor the Lancashire & Yorkshire was one of the more innovative lines. John Aspinall had been its locomotive superintendent in the last part of the century, and had produced a 2-4-2 tank locomotive whose suspension was carefully designed to enable it to tackle the fast medium-distance trains that were so numerous on the L & Y. Then his Atlantic express engines appeared in 1899. These still retained inside cylinders, and were indifferent steamers until they were superheated, but their massive boilers showed that Aspinall realized that steam production was the vital element in locomotives designed to pull trains that were becoming heavier and faster year by year. The final years of the L & Y locomotive department were in the hands of George Hughes, who was one of the rare designers who took theory seriously. It was his trials and calculations that convincingly demonstrated, to British engineers at least, that the extra capital and maintenance expenses of compound locomotives exceeded the value of their fuel economy. He built a four-cylinder 4-6-0 which, after superheating and redesign of its steam passages, did well.

The Great Northern had been served by a succession of very capable mechanical engineers. In 1895 Harry Ivatt was appointed, and he left his mark with his 4-4-2 express engines. The first variety was soon succeeded by a larger-boilered type, which put up performances normally associated with bigger engines, once it had been superheated. In 1911 Ivatt was succeeded by Nigel Gresley, who would remain in office with the GN's successor, the LNER, until 1941. In his time on the GN he introduced a 2-6-0, perhaps influenced by the GWR decision to favor that wheel arrangement over the 0-6-0. This design had a pony truck with a swing link devised by Gresley that made it an exceptionally smooth rider. Gresley soon discovered the virtues of three-cylinder configuration, and produced a 2-8-0 with three cylinders in which the valve gear of the central cylinder was actuated by levers from the outside cylinders. This 'derived' motion would become a hallmark of his locomotives; its advantage was space-saving in a very constricted part of the locomotive, while its drawback was that it demanded very careful maintenance. Another Gresley type was

a sturdy 0-6-2 tank for the heavy suburban trains out of Kings Cross and, just before the railway grouping, his first three-cylinder Pacific, *Great Northern*. This carried on the Ivatt tradition of big boilers, but it was more than just an enlargement of the previous Atlantic. It was essentially a prototype, that had great scope for development.

The Great Central had the good fortune to have as its locomotive superintendent J.G. Robinson, once described as 'one of the most successful designers of the British hit-or-miss school.' He probably did not grasp the importance of the relationships between various parameters, although he did appreciate the need for large boilers and had a useful preference for simplicity. His 'Director' inside-cylinder 4-4-0s were excellent, but his 4-6-0s, of

Below: *The Great Marquess, of a 2-6-0 design introduced by the LNER for the hilly West Highland line in 1937.*

Inset: *A former Great Eastern Railway 0-6-0 now working on a preserved line.*

Above: *SR locomotives at Bodmin in Cornwall; a Maunsell 2-6-0 leaves with a London train while a former LSWR 2-4-0 tank engine shunts in the yard.*

Left: *A mixed-traffic 4-6-0 designed by Urie for the LSWR, and with the LSWR high-capacity tender, with a semi-fast train at Basingstoke.*

Above: A pair of small 0-4-4 tank locomotives built for the LSWR doublehead a branch train at Bere Alston in Devon.

which he built half a dozen different varieties in small batches, were mediocre, largely because the air passages to their grates were too constricted. He achieved his peak with a 2-8-0 freight locomotive, which was so good that it was built for military service in World War One, being known as the ROD (Railway Operating Division) type. This locomotive, although resembling the 4-6-0s, was unlike them in that it produced an abundance of steam; firemen used to joke that a burning rag placed in the firebox would cause the safety valves to blow. At the time of the railway grouping Robinson was offered the post of chief mechanical engineer of the new LNER. Modestly, he declined, and the job went to Gresley who, otherwise, would not have had a chance to build his subsequent record-breaking Pacifics.

As for the Great Eastern, this had one of the most conservative of locomotive departments, with strong reliance on 4-4-0 and 0-6-0 types. When James Holden's 4-4-0 was enlarged by his son and successor Stephen Holden to an inside-cylinder 4-6-0, however, the result was far more successful than such enlargements on other railways. After the grouping some of these Holden 4-6-0s were actually drafted to the lines of the former Great North of Scotland Railway, whose overlong reliance on light 4-4-0s had created a minor motive power crisis; the low axleweight of the GER 4-6-0 made it exceptionally suitable for this role.

The London & South Western was interesting in that it employed the somewhat conservative and rough Drummond as locomotive superintendent, sandwiched between the reigns of two more sensitive men. William Adams, locomotive superintendent until 1895, had made several useful inventions and had been one of the few to favor outside cylinders for passenger locomotives. Drummond reverted to inside cylinders, opposed superheating, and was unable to enlarge his 4-4-0s into successful 4-6-0s. When his rule came to an end after he was lethally scalded by locomotive steam, he was succeeded by R.W. Urie, who did make the successful leap to the 4-6-0, which he built in three varieties, with different driving wheel diameters. Those with the larger, 6 foot 7 inch wheels became the first batch of 'King Arthurs,' a fast passenger design later perpetuated with great success by the Southern Railway. For its suburban traffic the LSWR relied heavily on the 0-4-4 tank engine, a type that Drummond had favored during his earlier career on the Caledonian.

The LBSCR, with its high-frequency, short-distance services, used a large number of tank locomotives. One of these, a 4-4-2, was one of the first locomotives to be superheated and in a trial over the LNWR ran from London to Rugby without taking water, a feat so astonishing that the LNWR immediately adopted superheating for its own loco-

motives. The LBSCR also owned some small 4-4-0s, still operated 0-4-2s, and in its last years introduced a successful 2-6-0, some large 4-6-2 and 4-6-4 tank engines, and Atlantics of the Great Northern design.

The SECR locomotive department until 1913 was in the hands of H.S. Wainwright, who was more interested in rolling stock design than locomotives. He had a fine aesthetic sensibility and the 'Wainwright 4-4-0,' in whose fundamental design he probably played only a minor part, was probably the best-looking engine of that wheel arrangement in Britain. He was succeeded by a very different man, Richard Maunsell. Delegating much design work to subordinates who had worked under Churchward on the GWR, Maunsell was the first locomotive designer to apply Churchward principles. In his 2-6-0 he probably surpassed Churchward for, while adopting the Churchwardian wheel arrangement, Belpaire firebox, tapered boiler and long-travel valves, he also used high-temperature superheat. The SECR 2-6-0 design was chosen by the government after World War One as a suitable type to be built by otherwise underemployed munitions works. A few were in fact built by Woolwich Arsenal and the type was used in Ireland as well as Southern England.

As for the self-styled 'Premier Line,' this had a far from premier locomotive stock. The long love-affair with compounding had left the LNWR at the turn of the century with locomotives that were well below

Top: *Another view of the 'Midland Compound' in its present, preserved, condition.*

Above: *One of the 0-4-4 tank locomotives built by the SECR for its suburban services.*

Right: *The SR inherited a numerous class of large 0-4-4 tank engines built for the LSWR suburban services. This is one of them, a class 'M7,' that has been preserved.*

the required capacity. In 1903 George Whale became locomotive superintendent and did his best to repair the damage. Very much an old broom, he swept back to the simple, robust, locomotive that had once typified the LNWR. His 4-4-0s of the 'Precursor' type were technically unexciting, and drivers had to thrash them, but they kept time with heavy trains. When his successor introduced a superheated version, the 'George the Fifths,' they were an immediate success even though they too needed to be worked excessively hard. Enlargements of the 4-4-0 to several varieties of inside cylinder 4-6-0 were reasonably successful, although not on the same plane as contemporary locomotives of the GWR, L&Y, GN or SECR. Whale's successor

introduced a more sophisticated 4-6-0, the four-cylinder 'Claughton' class which, once again because of restricted air passages, was a mediocre performer.

When the LMS was formed its two largest constituent companies, the LNWR and the Midland, already had motive power problems, although they were not willing to admit it. The MR's reliance on small engines was poor preparation for an age in which wage costs were likely to rise and train weights to increase. Not only did the MR depend on modest 4-4-0s for its passenger services, but its heavy freight trains, including an intense service of coal trains to London, depended on 0-6-0s, which increasingly had to be used in pairs. The LNWR,

Above: *One of the Stanier Class '5' mixed traffic locomotives at work near Cambridge.*

Left: Usk Castle, *one of the GWR's celebrated 'Castle' class, heads south from Birmingham with a London train.*

although having a good stock of 0-8-0 freight locomotives, had no passenger locomotives that could effortlessly deal with the trains expected in the 1920s. Luckily, the first chief mechanical engineer of the new company was neither an LNWR nor a Midland man, but George Hughes of the L & Y. Although he did not stay long, the mixed-traffic 2-6-0 that he bequeathed to the LMS was a very capable performer, even on express trains. However, the LMS still lacked a locomotive suitable for hauling fast heavy trains in the Anglo-Scottish service; while the rival East Coast Route already had large Pacifics the LMS depended on small 'Midland Compounds,' worn-out LNWR 4-4-0s, a few L & Y 4-6-0s, and LNWR 4-6-0s of far from splendid performance.

Hughes was followed, from 1925, by Henry Fowler, an engineer of wide rather than specialist capability who had been the MR's last locomotive superintendent. He had actually built a unique 0-10-0 engine for use on the Lickey Incline, so he was not totally addicted to small engines. But under

his regime other MR engineers and draughtsmen became influential, and MR practices were imposed. Additional 'Midland Compounds' and other MR 4-4-0s were ordered, and a compromise was reached over coal trains, which received big locomotives. The novel (for a British railway) step of ordering patent Beyer-Garratt locomotives was agreed. These locomotives, which consisted essentially of two locomotive chassis with a pivoted boiler spanning the gap between them, were popular in the British Empire as they provided the equivalent of two locomotives on a low axleweight and needed only a single crew. But MR engineers imposed their own detail standards on these locomotives, and in particular the steam distribution was old-fashioned and skimpy. So although the Garratts did what they were designed to do, they did not do it splendidly.

Fowler actually designed a 4-6-2, a compound using experience with the compound 4-4-0, but it was never built, probably because so many former MR men, especially the civil engineers, objected to

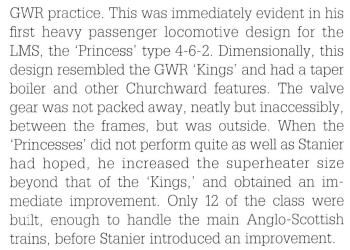

Left: Stanier's first 4-6-2 design, the 'Princess' class, which in many ways followed GWR practice.

Below: A GWR 'Hall,' the very successful mixed traffic 4-6-0 that inspired Stanier to design his Class '5.'

the very idea of a big locomotive. So when the LMS management decided it needed to match the LNER, it went to an outside builder, North British, which produced for it the 'Royal Scot' class 4-6-0.

Eventually the LMS management decided to appoint a chief mechanical engineer whose background was not with one of the constituent companies, and William Stanier of the GWR was appointed. Some years previously the LMS had tried out a GWR 'Castle,' and had been much impressed by its performance. However, the GWR management had not been keen to lend the drawings and the 'Royal Scots' were built instead. Appointing Stanier seemed a good and cheap way of acquiring Great Western technology. And so it turned out; Stanier not only introduced the best of Swindon practice, but improved on it. He had spent several years as a GWR locomotive operator, and had learned the weak as well as the strong points of

GWR practice. This was immediately evident in his first heavy passenger locomotive design for the LMS, the 'Princess' type 4-6-2. Dimensionally, this design resembled the GWR 'Kings' and had a taper boiler and other Churchward features. The valve gear was not packed away, neatly but inaccessibly, between the frames, but was outside. When the 'Princesses' did not perform quite as well as Stanier had hoped, he increased the superheater size beyond that of the 'Kings,' and obtained an immediate improvement. Only 12 of the class were built, enough to handle the main Anglo-Scottish trains, before Stanier introduced an improvement.

This improved design was the 'Princess Coronation' class, later known as the 'Duchesses.' Introduced in 1937 for the new 'Coronation Scot' train, they were streamlined, had larger boilers than the 'Princesses,' slightly larger driving wheels and more open steam passages. 38 of these engines, regarded by some as the finest passenger locomotives ever built in Britain, were produced. The first unit, *Coronation*, appeared at a time when the LMS and LNER were engaged in a well-publicized rivalry, and its alleged achievement of 114 mph on trial was considered a great success, because an LNER Pacific had recently set a record of 112 mph. This competition for maximum speed was somewhat unfair, as the LMS did not have a stretch of line comparable with the LNER's for attempting speed records. It was the LNER which would set the final record. However, one of the Stanier locomotives did achieve a record power output while hauling a 600-ton train up Beattock Bank on the Scottish main line, 3300 indicated horsepower being registered.

Meanwhile, Stanier designed and built several other new classes, to replace the older pre-grouping engines. For the lighter express services he built the 'Jubilee' three-cylinder 4-6-0s, but probably his most successful type was the class '5' 4-6-0, a mixed-traffic engine that was an improved version of the GWR 'Hall', and of which over 800 units were eventually built. It was an immediately successful type, and many of its components were used for a 2-8-0 freight engine, the '8F.' Yet another highly successful design was a 2-6-4 tank engine for outer suburban trains. By the late 1930s Stanier's design work was mainly finished, his assistants being entrusted with most new work. They rebuilt the 'Royal Scots' on Stanier lines, and these three-cylinder 4-6-0s, with virtually new engines, were outstandingly successful. The process was later extended to the 'Patriot' class. The latter 4-6-0 design had originated as a Midland-style rebuild of the mediocre LNWR 'Claughtons,' and the result had been satisfactory rather than electrifying. But, given taper boilers and improved steam passages, their performance became almost equal to that of the rebuilt 'Royal Scots.'

Above left: A 'Grange' leaves Swansea with a train for West Wales in the 1950s.

Lower left: A London to Pembroke Dock train leaves Swansea behind a 'Hall' locomotive that has replaced the 'Castle' that hauled it from London.

Above: Sir Meliagrance of the SR's 'King Arthur' class brings a stopping train into Basingstoke.

The GWR designs which so influenced Stanier were mainly those by Charles Collett, who had succeeded Churchward as chief mechanical engineer of the Great Western. Collett contented himself with enlarging and improving Churchward designs, but by taking a 'Saint' 4-6-0 and exchanging its 6 foot 8 inch driving wheels for smaller 6 foot wheels, he produced a highly competent mixed-traffic locomotive which eventually, as the 'Hall' class, exceeded 300 units. Somewhat smaller mixed-traffic locomotives, the 'Grange' and 'Manor' classes with 5 foot 8 inch drivers, followed.

But Collett's greatest success was the 'Castle' class of four-cylinder 4-6-0. This was simply an enlargement of Churchward's 'Star' class, but its slight increment of power was all that was needed to create a record-breaking class. While it is their work on fast trains like the 'Cheltenham Flyer' which is best remembered, these were engines which in the 1940s proved capable of regularly hauling 13-coach trains on fast schedules. When, after World War Two, they were given bigger superheaters and double chimneys, their performance was even better. In the late 1920s a further enlargement of the type, with a higher boiler pressure and slightly smaller driving wheels, produced the 30-strong 'King' class. This was probably not as fast-running as the 'Castles', but its extra power made it ideal for hauling heavy trains over the London to Plymouth and London to Wolverhampton routes with their tough climbs, respectively, up the Dainton and Hatton banks. But the 'Kings,' 'Castles' and 'Halls,' all

introduced in the 1920s, really represented the peak of GWR achievement. Henceforth it was a matter of resting on Churchward's laurels, until at the very end of the steam era Swindon research produced further advances in locomotive exhaust and draughting design.

On the LNER, Nigel Gresley built a further series of Pacifics of the same design as his *Great Northern*, and in 1925 he borrowed *Pendennis Castle* for trials. This GWR engine outperformed his Pacifics, and Gresley quickly imitated some of the GWR features: long-travel valves and higher boiler pressure. He also provided bigger superheaters and, after these modifications, found that he had produced a superb design. One of these engines, *Flying Scotsman*, ran from London to Leeds with a light four-coach trial train at an average of 73 mph. Another, *Papyrus*, averaged 100mph over 12 miles down Stoke Bank. These speed achievements encouraged Gresley in his design of an even faster Pacific, his streamlined A4 type. This was similar to the previous class, but had higher boiler pressure and more generous internal steam passages. Designed initially for hauling the new 'Silver Jubilee' train, the A4 was an immediate success. *Silver Link*, the first to be built, reached 112 mph on trial and another, *Mallard*, reached 126 mph, thereby setting an unbeaten record for steam traction.

A scaled-down version of the Gresley Pacific soon appeared for fast freights and fast passenger work. This was the V2, which had the unusual wheel arrangement of 2-6-2, and which achieved a high reputation; when in good condition this type could deputize for the Pacifics. Gresley was not afraid of innovation. His *Cock o' the North* was a 2-8-2 designed for heavy passenger trains in Scotland, and he also designed a light 2-6-2 for secondary lines. His K3 2-6-0, thanks to its typically large GN boiler, was a successful mixed-traffic engine. But his preference for three cylinders, with the middle cylinder regulated by a derived valve gear, meant that his locomotives needed careful maintenance, a requirement that was difficult to meet after 1939.

On the smallest of the new companies, the Southern Railway, locomotive policy was affected by the commitment to electrification. But although the various classes were built in much smaller numbers than on the other railways, variations within classes were numerous because Maunsell, the chief mechanical engineer until 1937, was a man ever willing to try out new ideas. For the SR he brought out new variations of the successful 2-6-0 he had designed for the SECR, varying the size of driving wheel and also building some with three cylinders. A tank locomotive version of this design, the 'River' class, was very good but after one was involved in a

fatal derailment the class was converted to tender locomotives. For heavy passenger work Maunsell took the existing LSWR 4-6-0, and improved its draughting and valve travel to form the 'King Arthur' class, an unspectacular design that always seemed capable of doing more than it was designed to do. For the most difficult passenger services he built sixteen of his 'Lord Nelson' four-cylinder 4-6-0s and then, using components of the 'King Arthur' and 'Lord Nelson' classes, he produced his masterpiece, the 'Schools.' These were of a wheel arrangement that was regarded as obsolescent, 4-4-0, but they performed far better than any previous 4-4-0s. In fact, they were probably the equal of the 'King Arthurs' despite their smaller size. They had three cylinders, and the cranks were set so that there would be six exhausts per revolution; this smoothed

Above Left: Lord Nelson, *Maunsell's powerful 4-6-0 for the Southern Railway.*

Above: *The LNER* Flying Scotsman *in its present-day role of excursion train haulage.*

Left: Christ's Hospital *of the 'Schools' class makes a heavy start from Redhill.*

Overleaf: *After the Great War Vickers, like several armaments firms, took a short-lived interest in locomotives.*

the torque, enabling a high power output to be achieved without the wheel-slip that would otherwise have resulted at full power. Forty 'Schools' were built, which for the SR was a large number.

Maunsell was succeeded by Oliver Bulleid, whose highly novel designs for an 0-6-0 and a 4-6-2 would only appear after the most glamorous age of steam had come to an end in September 1939. In the few years before the war he improved the performance of Maunsell's passenger engines by fitting large-diameter 'Lemaitre' chimneys. Having worked under Gresley, Bulleid was full of ideas, and in due course got most of them out of his system.

When the interwar period ended, the four companies had established their own identities in the field of locomotive design. But although their locomotives looked very different, in fact they were the

outcome of the same history. All four companies had absorbed the lessons taught by Churchward about the importance of long valve travel and the advantage of higher boiler pressures. The LMS and LNER, and probably the SR too, had been influenced by the big-boiler philosophy practised by the Great Northern and Lancashire & Yorkshire railways. The GWR, partly because of conservatism and partly because it burned high-quality Welsh coal, was less addicted to big boilers and it did not appreciate the value of high-temperature superheat as practised by the other companies. The importance of a good exhaust arrangement to provide a firm draught for the fire and to eliminate back-pressure in the cylinders had been realized by the LNER, LMS and SR, and each of these companies had installed double or wide diameter chimneys.

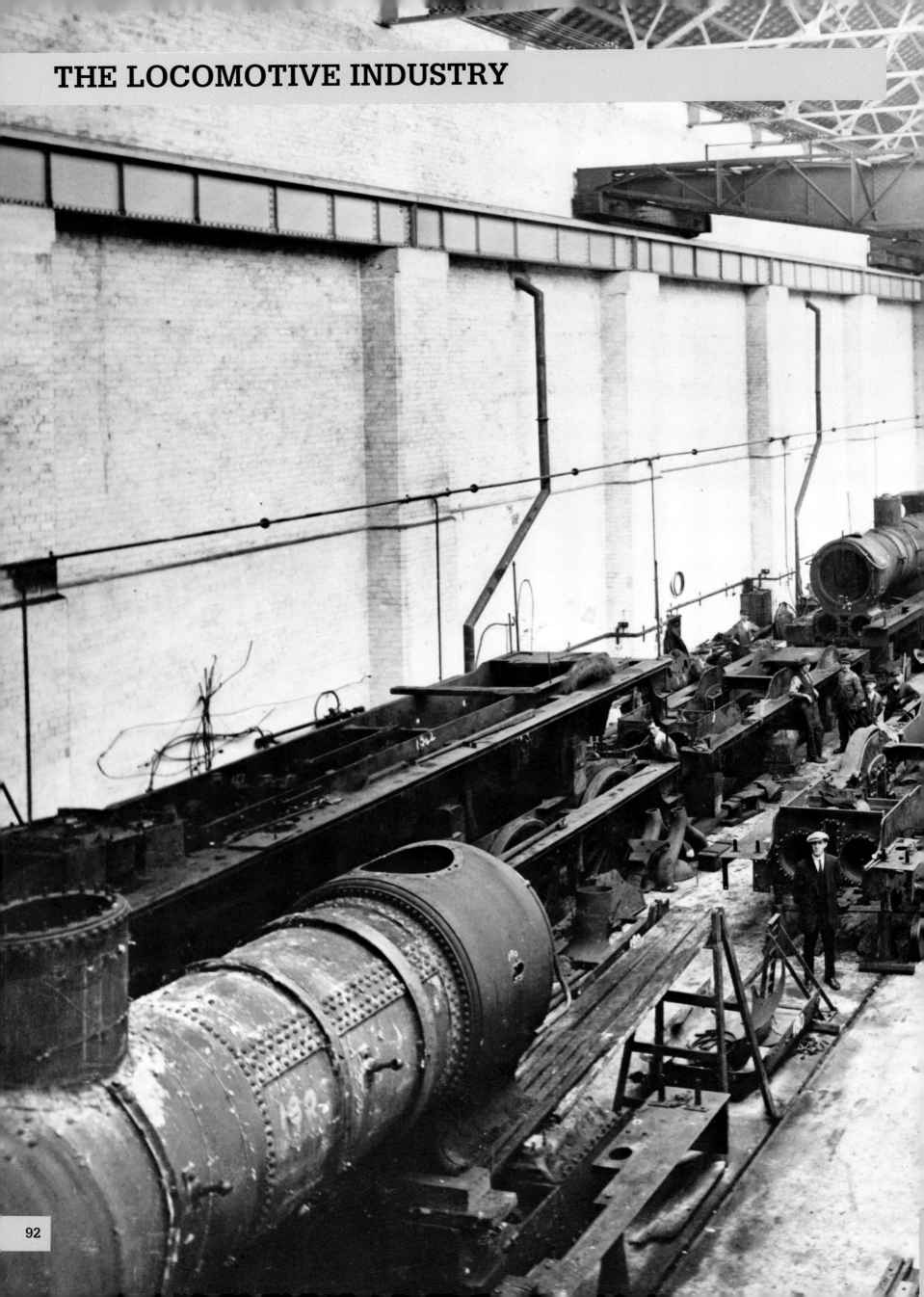

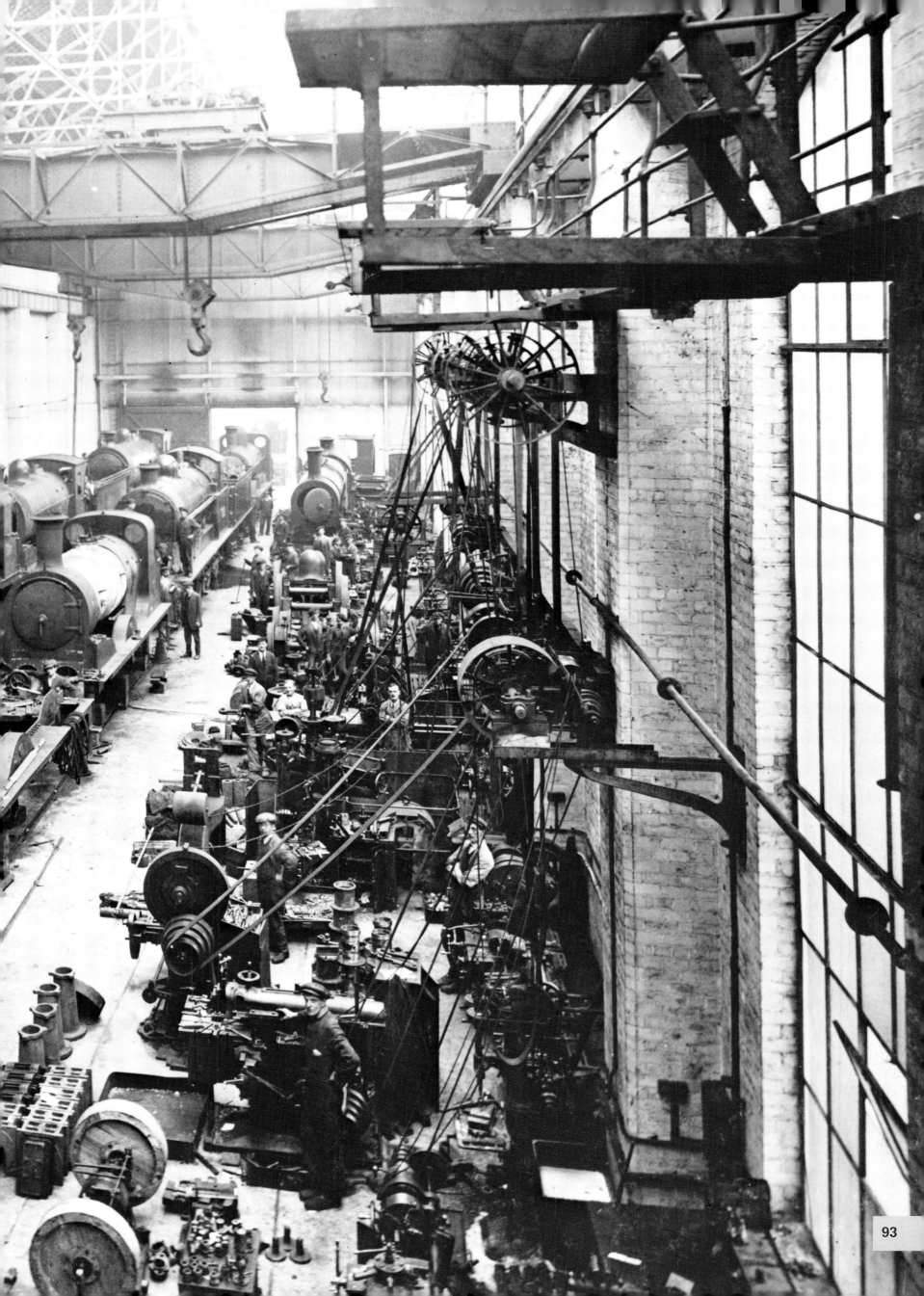

Left: *The three lives of a locomotive design. This first picture is of an LMS 'Patriot,' formerly a 'Claughton,' in its final rebuilt form as a 'Baby Scot,' with new taper boiler.*

Lower left: *The original and somewhat mediocre 'Claughton' design of the LNWR. This is* Sir Gilbert Laughton *hauling a London-Glasgow express in 1913.*

Below: *The 'Patriot' design, which was the LMS rebuild of the original 'Claughton' type.*

Among industrial countries Britain was peculiar in that it had not one, but two distinct locomotive industries. The original industry developed from the contractors who built locomotives for the first railway companies. Some of these contractors, poorly equipped and with little commercial or engineering talent, soon returned to simpler products but a few of the others developed into large locomotive factories which, in due course, learned to cooperate as well as compete and became members of their own trade association.

The other locomotive industry consisted of the workshops of the different railway companies. Originally these workshops were for the repair of locomotives and rolling stock and were managed by superintendents who had, usually, some experience of locomotive-building in the works of the locomotive contractors. Once appointed to supervise the running and repair of a railway's locomotive stock they soon developed the ambition to design and build locomotives themselves. In this they were encouraged by their managements, who anticipated not only a saving of money but better designs and prompter delivery. At that time Britain really was the workshop of the world, and the locomotive contractors were so loaded with orders from home and abroad that their deliveries were not always prompt, nor their prices and designs the best that might be obtained.

After all, the assembly of a completely new locomotive was not all that different from the heavy repair of an existing locomotive, and could be carried out in the same workshop. This remained true right up to the end of steam traction, despite the growing size of locomotives. Heavy repairs involved among other things, the exchange of boilers, and the cranes that could lift boilers were sufficient to perform the other lifts involved in locomotive construction. Similarly, the workshops for boiler repair required no alterations, just the provision of plate-bending equipment if it was not already installed. Materials and specialized components could be bought in from outside suppliers, although as time passed the locomotive works tended to produce more and more of their own components and even, occasionally, basic materials like steel.

The erection of a new locomotive took little longer than a heavy repair. In fact, if repairs were organized inefficiently, it could take less. Crewe set a record in 1878 by assembling a locomotive in 25 hours, but this was a special effort involving a simple 0-6-0 engine with which the works already had much experience. In the 1930s, an LMS Pacific needed three weeks, while simpler and smaller engines took less.

Such times presupposed a very efficient work organization, so that the components became available at exactly the right moment. Late components could hold up the program, while early deliveries caused congestion and higher costs. Except when new designs were introduced, it was usual to order locomotives from the works in batches, in accordance with the annual investment plan approved by the company directors. With new designs it was customary to build just one or two units at first, postponing batch production until they had been tried out. On occasions when this was not done, there was the risk of expensive post-production modifications or, worse, the construction of a class whose performance was disappointing. The GWR's only Pacific locomotive, *The Great Bear*, was an example of the wise approach. Only one was built, and its trials showed that it was not a design the GWR needed.

With batches of existing designs, it was usual to order the long-lead items six or more months in

advance. These were the boilers and fireboxes, which were put together in the clamorous boiler shop. This built the boiler and firebox, but the fittings were installed separately. Hundreds of feet of tubing were fitted, mostly in the form of the internal boiler tubes. Then there were other necessary components, including the safety valves and the regulator. The finished boiler was then subjected to several trials, including a hydraulic and one or two steam pressure tests. Such testing, which involved pressures considerably higher than the boiler's nominal rating, had become more thorough over the decades. In smaller works in the nineteenth century such testing was less thorough, but as boiler pressures were then lower this does not imply that the boilers of that time were unsafe. The last stage of a boiler's construction was lagging and the fitting of its outer sheeting. Lagging was typically with asbestos and it was not until after the steam era that the health hazards, both of asbestos and the ear-splitting din of boilershops, were recognized.

Frame plates, the foundation of a completed engine, were ordered about a month after the boiler. They were about an inch thick and in the later decades of locomotive-building were cut out from steel slabs with oxyacetylene blowpipes, before being machined on a slotting machine that drilled the holes needed for attaching the various parts of the engine. The cylinders, in particular, had to be firmly bolted on. Casting cylinders was one of the most difficult assignments of the works foundry, carried out in a cooperative effort by patternmakers, moulders, and core-makers. After the casting, the cylinders required much intricate finishing work before being bolted on to the frames.

Steel wheel centers were cast, and machined in the wheel shop, then forced on to the axles in a hydraulic press. The tyres were added to these centers after heating; this increased their diameter by about one-sixteenth of an inch; they could then be forced on to the wheel centers and, in cooling, contracted to impose a very tight grip. Meanwhile the machine shop was fabricating axleboxes, and drop-hammers were shaping coupling and connecting rods made of high-tensile steel. About 6000 rivets would be made and fitted in the construction of a large engine, and there were numerous other lathe products to be made.

Actual erection of the engine began when the frames were positioned in the erecting shop, and carefully aligned. Then, piece by piece, the components were brought in and bolted into position.

Above: *Sunday morning at the Motherwell locomotive depot, 1951. Former Caledonian Railway locomotives dominate the scene though that company had disappeared almost 30 years previously.*

Above right: *The GWR pannier tank locomotive; at right the traditional pre-Churchward concept, and at left the final, Americanized, version.*

Right: *This GWR 'Castle' incorporated parts from the unsuccessful Pacific The Great Bear, whose number was also transferred.*

When all was assembled the locomotive was painted and then weighed, axle by axle. It was rare for the weight to be perfectly distributed between, say, the left hand and right hand wheels of a given axle, but small differences could be tolerated. After that, the engine was fired up, static tests made and, finally, it was taken out for its trial run.

By the twentieth century all the large railway companies were building their own locomotives to their own individual designs and specifications. When traffic expansion required more new locomotives than they could build themselves, they ordered locomotives of their own design from one or more of the contract builders. The latter, denied the major share of locomotive building for the home railways, had by this time concentrated on the export market, and in particular on designing and building locomotives for the railways of the British Commonwealth.

Locomotive design was another aspect that the two sides of the industry handled differently. The railway-owned workshops were headed by each company's 'locomotive carriage and wagon superintendent' (the title 'chief mechanical engineer' was substituted in the twentieth century). This engineer was responsible for design, production, and repair, and it often happened that an engineer who was

quite undistinguished for locomotive design could yet be a priceless asset to his company by virtue of originality and efficiency in production engineering. It was sometimes quite difficult to determine who was the real designer of a locomotive type. The chief mechanical engineer might simply decide on a specification and leave it to his draughtsmen to produce drawings. The most notable engineers tended to give great responsibility to their chief draughtsmen, but contrived to spend much of their time in the drawing office and to take a personal part in working out the details of the innovations they introduced.

In the contract factories, things were organized rather differently with, typically, the chief draughtsman being the key figure in design. As the decades passed more and more of the overseas railways ordering British-built locomotives chose to send in their own designs, or at least outlines, rather than leave design to the locomotive works. This process

Below: *Evolution of the Beyer Peacock look, with inclined cylinders and unchanging design of details. This loco class was supplied to New South Wales in the 1870s.*

Right: *An earlier Beyer Peacock design, supplied to the Isle of Man. See page 151 for a later and larger Beyer Peacock design, still retaining the family resemblance.*

was never complete, and most locomotive works did produce their own designs which, quite often, would be simultaneously purchased by railways in different countries. It was the larger railway systems, like those of Australia and South Africa, which tended to work out their own outline designs, and then get the British works to build them. Locomotive designers in the contract side of the locomotive industry never gained the public celebrity enjoyed by British railway company engineers like Gresley, Stanier, or Churchward.

By the turn of the century there were about ten large contract builders, each employing more than 300 workers, and several smaller ones. The latter tended to concentrate on small locomotives and small production runs whereas the larger companies were prepared to tackle anything. The biggest company was Neilson, with more than 3000 workers, and in 1903 it joined forces with two other big companies, Dubs and Sharp Stewart, to form the North British Locomotive Company. Holding a dominant position in the market, NBL built over 11,000 locomotives for home and overseas railways before its demise in 1962. The three constituent factories were located close together in the Springburn district of Glasgow.

Another important company was Beyer Peacock, established in Gorton (Manchester) not far from the locomotive works of the Great Central Railway. Founded by a German in 1854, the company produced locomotives of excellent workmanship and graceful, rounded, lines. Its preference for outside cylinders, inclined downwards, was exemplified in many designs of the late nineteenth century, including tank locomotives for London's Metropolitan Railway and several designs for New South Wales, where the company was the favored supplier. In the twentieth century it acquired the patent for the Garratt locomotive, which was virtually two engines in one and used by railways that could accept its higher maintenance costs in exchange for its low axleweight and high power.

Two companies dating back to the earliest days of railways were among the ten biggest works in the twentieth century. One of them was Robert Stephenson, descended from the factory that built the *Rocket*. By 1900 it employed 800 men and was about to move from its ancestral home in Newcastle to more spacious premises at Darlington. In the 1930s it absorbed other companies and survived the end of steam construction to become part of the English Electric group in 1962. Another works having Robert Stephenson as founder was the Vulcan Foundry, which produced over 6000 locomotives from 1833 to the end of steam.

Of the railway-owned locomotive works, Swindon of the GWR and Crewe of the LNWR were per-

haps the best known. This fame owed something to the circumstance that they were both of early origin and both contributed very much to locomotive design, while belonging to big companies. Another feature they had in common was that they were both 'green field' enterprises, having been set down in quiet settlements that quite soon became big railway towns.

Unlike other industries, which were located close to their raw material or labor supply, works like Crewe and Swindon, being originally intended for repair, were sited at junctions with good access to the whole of their railway systems. Materials could easily be shipped in, and when the local labor supply was exhausted new workers could be attracted by the promise of jobs which, at that time, seemed stable, well-paid, and prestigious. Both at Crewe

Above: GWR 4-6-0 engines, being run in after going through works, inside Swindon locomotive shed.

Below: Goldfinch, *an Edwardian 4-4-0 with characteristic Swindon features including sharply tapered boiler, conical safety valve cover, and copper-capped chimney.*

Bottom: *Engines awaiting scrap at Swindon. The main works building is in the background.*

and Swindon, as well as at several other railway towns, social facilities were provided by the railway companies. These included housing, which was usually well in advance of working class housing in other towns, and water and sewage services. Public baths were provided and, almost always, a mechanics' institute which served as meeting place, assembly hall, library and evening school.

Swindon Works was built in 1842, but steadily expanded until at its peak it occupied 140 acres, of which 35 were covered by buildings. Apart from the erecting shop, where locomotives were built or underwent heavy repairs, there was a boiler shop and various workshops for cutting, rolling, and pressing steel, making castings in iron and brass, fabricating springs, and also supplying other departments. By the 1920s the works employed about

14,000 workers. It dominated the town, whose first mayor after it became a borough was George Churchward, the GWR locomotive superintendent.

In its early decades it was the bastion of the broad-gauge interest, and the successful effort made to prove that broad-gauge locomotives were better than standard-gauge no doubt helped to set it on the road to excellence in design and workman-ship. The gauge problem also meant that the GWR was peculiar in that it had two main locomotive works, Swindon for broad gauge and Wolverhampton to build and repair locomotives for its standard-gauge lines. In fact, after the GWR became a purely standard-gauge railway in the 1890s it seemed likely that Wolverhampton, not Swindon, would become the sole locomotive works. It was only the shortage

Above: *The builder's plate attached to locomotives built by Neilson.*

Top right: *The Vulcan Foundry works plate.*

Lower right: *The works plate used by Swindon for locomotives of BR design.*

at Wolverhampton of land for expansion that prevented this, and Wolverhampton built its last new engine in 1908. For some years, locomotives of the same class were built simultaneously at both works, and there were recognizable differences in the shape of the chimneys and the paintwork (Swindon used leaf green whereas Wolverhampton preferred a dark kind of bluish green).

Until the Churchward era GWR locomotives tended to be graceful and rounded, with a well-fed look about them. Then came the distinctive lean locomotives that set the pattern for the later 'Kings' and 'Castles.' Yet even in its last years Swindon also produced locomotives of essentially nineteenth century designs, and notably several classes of big-domed tank locomotives for branchline and shunt-

Above: *GWR locomotives of the Churchward era; a 2-6-2 tank engine leads a 2-8-0 into the Severn Tunnel.*

Right: *A typical LNWR product from Crewe; a 0-6-2 tank engine in service as station pilot at Birmingham New Street.*

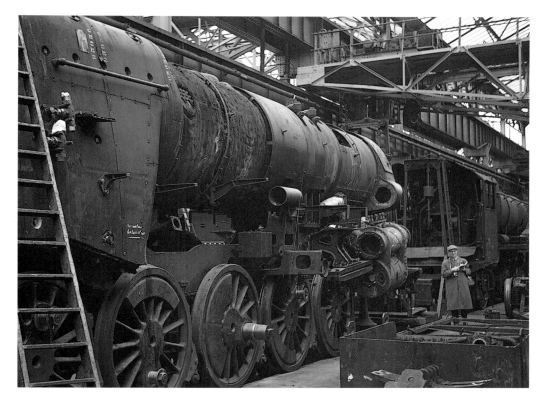

Top: *BR 2-10-0 locomotives under construction at Crewe in 1966.*

Above: *One of a class of 25 0-6-0 engines supplied by Neilson to the Argentine in 1888.*

parison with their Swindon-built contemporaries, but were cheaper to build and maintain, and whose rugged construction guaranteed a long life. Later, when it served the LMS, it was the source of Stanier's new range of standard locomotives, including his streamliners.

In the last half of the nineteenth century, and especially under the regime of Francis Webb, Crewe seemed determined to make everything the LNWR needed. It was a pioneer in the use of Bessemer steel, produced rails, signaling equipment, station furniture, artificial limbs, footwarmers, and many other items. Other locomotive works tended to spread into non-locomotive production, but not to the same extent as Crewe. A feature of most locomotive works was the attention paid to recycling old materials and components as a way of reducing costs. At Crewe, even soap was manufactured, using grease recovered from enginemens' cleaning rags. In the 1870s Crewe attempted to enter the locomotive market; its capacity at times exceeded the LNWR requirements and its costs were low, so it began to supply engines to another company, the Lancashire & Yorkshire. This was correctly seen as a threat by the contract locomotive-building companies, who joined together to oppose this transaction and succeeded in obtaining an injunction that prevented this practice.

William Ramsbottom, the inventive locomotive superintendent who invented, among other things, water troughs, was also responsible for imposing some kind of order and efficiency in Crewe Works during his term of office in 1857-71. But practices declined thereafter, even though locomotive design and construction improved. On the eve of the railway grouping, larger engines might spend two months at Crewe for heavy repairs, and on the LNWR as a whole about a quarter of the locomotive stock at any time might be under or awaiting repairs. When Hughes came from the L & Y he immediately attempted to improve efficiency, but the old guard of Crewe traditionalists resisted. However, his efforts were noticed by the younger generation of Crewe engineers, and the LMS works were eventually reorganized. Hughes also tried to introduced greater accuracy in manufacture, and managed to have micrometers accepted as one means of achieving this. In the 1930s Stanier insisted on finer precision; better finishing and machining brought an immediate reward in a decreased incidence of overheated axleboxes.

The LMS also built new locomotives at Derby, the works of the former Midland Railway. Although these Works were smaller than Crewe, covering 47 acres in 1900, they were older, having been built as early as 1840 although the first new locomotive was not turned out until 1851. From all accounts, Derby

ing duties. Many of these had square 'pannier' tanks, a Swindon speciality that combined larger water capacity with easy access to the cylinders and valve gear. Swindon's final design of shunting tank engine,however, at last combined old and new; it had a taper boiler and also an American feature that Churchward had not adopted – outside valve gear.

In the interwar years there was considerable investment in modern equipment, and Swindon became known for the fine tolerances with which its locomotives were assembled. There was little that was fine about Crewe tolerances but, in its own way, that works made its own contribution to the British locomotive tradition. Under LNWR ownership, Crewe Works succeeded in building locomotives that might perhaps have been unrefined in com-

was a good place to work, and the facilities provided for its personnel were as good as those of any other railway town. The Company owned the gasworks, built the Midland Railway Institute, and provided three canteens, of which one was for non-smokers. Around the turn of the century it was building about 40 new engines annually, and these included such celebrated types as the Midland 'Singles' and 'Compounds.' But, as with other locomotive works, its main task was repair, and about 750 locomotives passed through for heavy repairs each year. In the interwar years a new repair system was introduced, somewhat similar to a production line. Traditionally, a locomotive stayed in one place in the erecting shop, but under the new system it was moved forward for each phase of its repair, enabling specialist staff and equipment to be deployed most efficiently. This reduced the average time a locomotive spent at works, a crucially important index whose reduction enabled a railway to function with fewer locomotives. At Derby, before the introduction of the system, there were usually 200 to 300 locomotives in works, undergoing or awaiting repair. With the new system, this was reduced to an average of about 60. On the eve of nationalization a locomotive averaged only about 16 days in works, and a similar system

had been introduced at Crewe.

The LMS inherited Horwich Works, built by the Lancashire & Yorkshire Railway. This was the birthplace of some outstanding locomotives and also the training ground from rising engineers who went on to become mechanical engineers of other companies. John Aspinall, the L & Y's locomotive superintendent at the turn of the century, not only designed locomotives and went on to become an international railway celebrity, but also trained men who in the late 1920s would be the chief mechanical engineers of three of the four new mainline companies (Gresley of the LNER, Maunsell of the SR, and Fowler of the LMS). Another Horwich man, George Hughes, became the locomotive superintendent of the L & Y and subsequently of the new LMS, thereby enabling some of the advanced Horwich ideas to gain currency in the new larger company, and also postponing and thereby moderating the struggle between the MR and LNWR factions within the LMS mechanical engineering department.

Other locomotive-building works acquired by the LMS were limited to repair work. They included St Rollox in Glasgow, which had built locomotives for the Caldeonian Railway. Lochgorm Works of the Highland Railway had built engines only intermit-

Above: *The final, though not peak, example, of the Lancashire & Yorkshire Railway's Horwich Works passenger locomotive design was a class of 4-6-0. The last survivor is shown here, relegated to local freight work at Lytham.*

Above: *An example of a US design built by a British company. The Hunslet Company supplied this 'Andes' type 2-8-0 to Bolivia in 1948. In this picture its waste hot water is being snapped up by local people.*

Right: *A Gresley streamlined Pacific in works, with its outer casing removed.*

tently, the HR having ordered most of its loco-motives from contract builders. Kilmarnock Works of the Glasgow & South Western had been more ambi-tious, producing some good locomotives which, because of their small numbers, did not last for long after the railway grouping. This works, too was con-fined to repairs after the grouping. Bow Works in London, which had built tank locomotives for the North London Railway, also became repairs-only, while Stoke Works of the North Staffordshire Rail-way, being so close to Crewe, was closed in 1927.

The LNER on its formation inherited several medium-sized locomotive works. In terms of floor space, Gorton was the largest at 15 acres of covered area, closely followed by Doncaster at 13, Stratford with 12, and Darlington with 11 acres. It was Doncas-ter that was destined to become the most celebrated of the LNER works, for it was there that the Gresley Pacifics were built. It was originally the main work-

LNER policy for integrating the locomotive depart-ments of the constituent companies was very dif-ferent from that of the LMS, and did not seek to put an early end to the designs and traditions of the con-stituent companies in the interest of standardization and centralization. Thus Robinson's design of 'Director' 4-4-0 remained in production for use in Scotland, while the Gorton Works was entrusted, apart from new LNER designs, with the construc-tion of a suburban tank locomotive that had actually originated on the Great Eastern Railway.

The Great Eastern works had been at Stratford, but continued to build locomotives only until 1924, one of the final batches being ten 4-4-0 engines of the celebrated GER 'Claud Hamilton' series. From its beginning in 1854 to the final engine of 1924, Stratford had built about 1700 locomotives. The GER had never been a very prosperous company, but the elegant but robust outlines of its passenger loco-

shops of the GNR, and turned to locomotive con-struction only in the 1860s. By the 1890s it could pro-duce a hundred locomotives annually. Thanks to a succession of very competent locomotive super-intendents it became the birthplace of very success-ful locomotive designs, each of which seemed the natural successor of the previous design. In other words, there was a distinct Doncaster 'school' of de-sign visible from the Stirling 'Singles' to the Gresley Pacifics. In all, this works built about 2200 loco-motives and in the late 1940s was employing about 3000 workers.

Gorton Works in Manchester had been owned by the Great Central Railway, and its designs had in-cluded the celebrated 'ROD' 2-8-0. Its first loco-motive superintendent, Richard Peacock, became a co-founder of the contract builder Beyer Peacock in 1854 while its last superintendent, J.G.Robinson, was designer of the 'ROD' freight locomotive. The

Above: *A pair of Great Eastern 4-6-0s, rebuilt by the LNER, pull out of Cambridge.*

Right: *One of the variety of 4-4-2 engines designed by Robinson and built by the GCR's Gorton Works.*

Above left: *The MR 'Lickey Banker,' an exception to the Derby Works small engine policy.*

Left: *A 0-4-4 tank engine designed and built by the North Eastern Railway.*

motives, luxuriously turned out in dark glossy blue with ornate lettering, helped to disguise this state of affairs.

Darlington, the other big LNER locomotive works, had been established by the North Eastern Railway and produced its first steam locomotive in 1864; its last, the 2268th, was turned out in 1957. In the intervening years it had supplied the NER with a range of very sturdy locomotives, and in LNER times it shared in the production of Gresley's standard types; in the case of the three-cylinder 'Shire' 4-4-0, it built the entire class. Finally, under British Railways auspices, it reverted to a NER design when a light 0-6-0 tank locomotive was required.

The LNER's works in Scotland ceased new production soon after the grouping. In its time, Cowlairs Works of the North British Railway in Glasgow had been renowned for its sturdy, if conservative, products. Between 1844 and 1924 it built around 900 new locomotives, and these included the 'Scott' and 'Glen' 4-4-0 designs that lasted in passenger service up to the 1950s. Much smaller than Cowlairs was the Inverurie Works of the Great North of Scotland Railway. This was a small and frugal railway, and its

Above: *Ashford Works' builder's plate.*

Upper left: *Darlington Works' builder's plate, as fixed to an 0-8-0 built in 1918.*

Left: Slieve Gullion, *one of a class of five 4-4-0 engines built by the Great Northern Railway of Ireland in 1913.*

locomotive works was appropriately modest. In fact, this works only produced ten locomotives, the remainder being ordered from contract builders.

The Southern Railway inherited three locomotive-building works, of which the most modern was Eastleigh, near Southampton. This works had been built by the London & South Western Railway in 1909 to replace its cramped works at Nine Elms, London. It had a spacious site of 41 acres, of which 11 were covered, and became the main works of the SR. Its output was quite small, totaling 320 engines during its life as a steam locomotive works. These engines did include some very notable designs, including the 'King Arthurs,' 'Lord Nelsons,' and 'Schools.' Later, the first Bulleid Pacifics were built there.

The oldest of the SR locomotive works was at Brighton. Built in 1840, it was remarkable for several reasons, the first being that a commuting and seaside resort like Brighton was an unlikely site for a locomotive works. Secondly, because it lay alongside Brighton Station the works was practically inaccessible to road vehicles. Finally, the site was so small (nine acres) that almost all of it (seven acres) was occupied by buildings; there was no room here for outside dumps or for expansion. When it belonged to the London Brighton & South Coast Railway the works built some elegant locomotives, rendered even more eye-catching by the yellow livery that the Railway favored for many years. Its 'Gladstone' 0-4-2 type had a high reputation, although that wheel arrangement was highly unorthodox for an express locomotive. Having a main line that was short but busy, the Company was something of a specialist in tank locomotives, and towards the end of its life was building massive 4-6-4 and 4-6-2 tank engines for heavy passenger trains. It had a comparatively small requirement for tender locomotives, its 'Brighton Atlantics' numbering only eleven units. As an SR works, Brighton shared in the building programme of the 1920s, but was withdrawn from locomotive production in the 1930s. However, in World War Two it was used to assemble Stanier 8F locomotives ordered by the government. Having few manufacturing facilities of its own, it imported the main components from Eastleigh and Ashford, and was able to erect a locomotive at the rate of one every five days. This technique was followed in the postwar years, when it was building Bulleid Pacifics. It closed in 1958.

Ashford Works was almost as old as Brighton, and build its first locomotive for the South Eastern Railway in 1853. Later it became the main works for the combined South Eastern & Chatham Railway. Its locomotives tended to be unglamorous but reliable, although the 'Wainwright 4-4-0' had many admirers. After Wainwright, Maunsell was the locomotive superintendent, and it was he who became chief mechanical engineer of the new SR. His very successful 2-6-0 for the SECR continued to be built at Ashford for the SR, but in 1944 locomotive construction ceased there with the final Ashford batch of standard wartime 8F engines.

Maunsell was one of several British locomotive engineers who had done a spell in one of the Irish locomotive works, in his case Inchicore Works at Dublin, which served the Great Southern & Western Railway and was the largest of the Irish works. Inchicore produced a large number of designs, but each was built in small numbers and tended to be unexciting in appearance and performance. An exception was the trio of 4-6-0s built for the Dublin-Cork mail trains in 1939, which bore a close resemblance to the LMS 'Rebuilt Scot' class. A smaller Irish works was at Broadstone, on the Dublin & South Eastern Railway, but construction ceased here in 1911. The Great Northern Railway of Ireland which, among other things, operated the key Belfast-Dublin line, had its works at Dundalk, and here were built an impressive series of relatively small (0-6-0 and 4-4-0) locomotives. Some of the interwar 4-4-0s were three-cylinder compounds, the last to be built in Britain.

Above left: *A Gresley 4-4-0, built at Darlington in the 1920s, draws a stopping train out of Edinburgh Waverley.*

Left: *A North British Railway 'Gien' 4-4-0, designed at Cowlairs Works.*

Above right: *One of Bulleid's 'Merchant Navy' Pacifics restarts its train from Basingstoke.*

Right: *A former LBSCR 2-6-0 awaits its turn for intermediate repairs at Brighton.*

Overleaf: *The driver and fireman of a resplendent GWR 'Star' pose proudly for the photographer in 1910.*

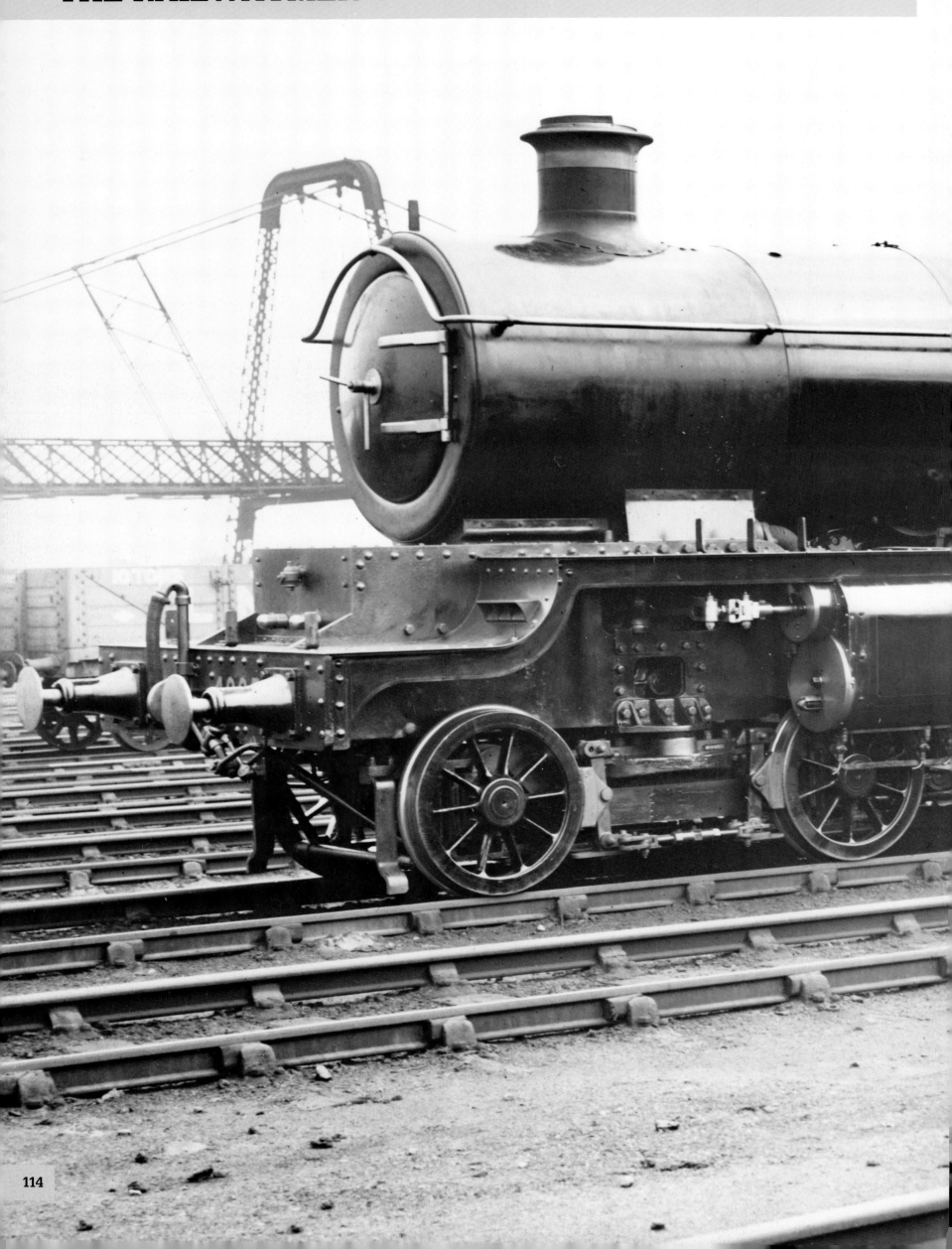

By the late 1840s the number of railwaymen had passed 50,000, and this figure grew rapidly so that in 1939, despite the Depression of the 1930s, there were about 600,000 workers and employees. Throughout that period the profession was highly prestigious, with applications for most jobs very much more numerous than the jobs available. This situation meant that, with the preference given to relatives of railwaymen, succeeding generations of families tended to enter railway service. Thus, quite apart from the professional solidarity engendered by the uniqueness of the calling, there were also strong family ties binding railwaymen together. This togetherness was reinforced by the pattern of housing. In railway towns, which could be former villages suddenly enlarged by becoming railway junctions or the sites of railway workshops, the companies usually built housing for their workers, which placed railway families together. Even in long-established cities the companies sometimes built blocks of flats for their workers near the terminals, and this had the same effect. In the countryside, stations were often provided with a block of terraced houses for the local staff, with one house being slightly grander than the others and reserved for the stationmaster.

It was a peculiar profession. It was more secure than most, because trains ran and needed workers whatever the state of the economy. At times of depression fewer freight trains were operated, but railway companies did not usually regard this as a

reason for shedding trained men who might be difficult to attract back when good times returned. On the other hand, men were quite often dismissed for misconduct or bad workmanship. Because the job was potentially dangerous and dependent on close cooperation, a worker who was unreliable got short shrift. If he began to fail through old age or injury, then the company usually did what it could to find a less demanding job, but if he was unpunctual, too fond of the bottle, or disobedient, then he was quickly dispensed with.

Railwaymen's solidarity, though real, was weakened by a kind of class division, with different grades of worker seeing themselves as distinctive, if not

Upper left: *The crew of a London Chatham & Dover Railway freight train.*

Left: *A wide-ranging sample of City and South London Railway staff in the early 1900s. A then rare species, the electric locomotive driver, is in the background.*

Above: *London & South Western Railway track workers and station staff at Ropley.*

elite. This division was reflected in the organization of trade unions, which began in the 1860s. By the standards of the time, the railway companies were good employers, but nevertheless they tried to keep wages low and to squeeze the maximum effort from their workers. The clerical staff were the first to form a union, followed by guards in combination with signalmen, and then by the locomotive men. The first strike to bring a company to a halt was on the LBSCR, where the unionized engine crews managed to secure a hearing for their demand for a wage rise. In the 1870s the Amalgamated Society of Railway Servants was formed with the object of uniting

all railway workers. Its Scottish affiliate, the ASRS of Scotland, was the first to organize a really major railway strike. This happened in 1890-91, when a demand for a ten-hour day and increased wages met with a sympathetic response from the public, who realized that long working hours were a cause of accidents. However, the Scottish ASRS leadership made the mistake of postponing its strike until the Christmas season, on the grounds that the more it hurt people the more pressure would be put on the companies. But this disruption of Hogmanay infuriated the Scottish public. The companies imported strike-breaking workers from England, some

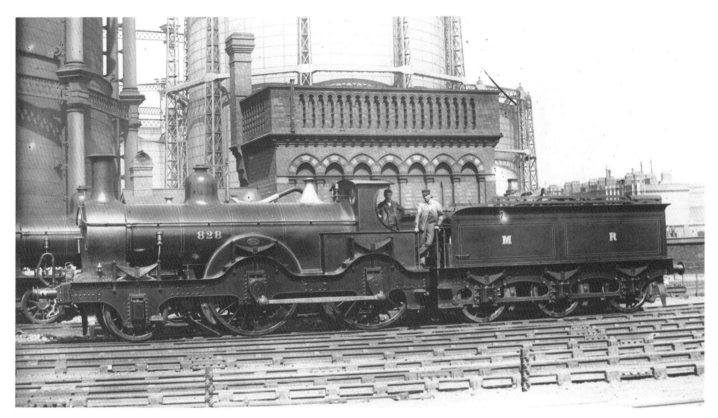

Left: *A Midland Railway engine crew take their engine past St Pancras gasworks in London.*

Below: *Turning a locomotive. The powered turntable was not universal, but was much appreciated.*

Right: *On the footplate of a Great Northern Atlantic.*

Lower right: *Mechanical overhead coaling plants were another advance that relieved workers of an unpleasant job, but they were comparatively rare.*

strikers resorted to violence, and the strike collapsed after six weeks. Another disastrous strike took place on the small Taff Vale Railway in 1900, when the workers demanded recognition of the union. This dispute was eventually resolved in the House of Lords, with the ASRS being required to pay the railway company substantial damages for loss of business. On the other hand, partly because of the rising strength of railway unionism, Parliament had become more willing to legislate on behalf of the railway workers, and the Board of Trade was given responsibility for supervising matters connected with safety, including the question of excessive working hours. The unions continued to struggle for recognition by the companies, and the railway strike of 1911 was partially successful in obtaining this.

The common object of keeping the trains running engendered a team spirit, but also required workers to turn out at all hours, to be away from home for long periods, to accept postings from one district to another and to do all this at wage rates

Above: *A 'Midland Compound' is given its weekly boiler wash-out.*

Left: *Locomotives under preparation for hauling suburban trains on the former London Tilbury & Southend Railway, later a part of the Midland Railway and then of the LMS.*

that, as the decades passed, declined relative to other professions. Whereas in the 1830s railways were so desperate to attract and to hold qualified workers that they paid high wages and tolerated individualism, this situation slowly changed. By the late 1940s the conditions of railway work, and the availability of better-paid and more comfortable work elsewhere, presented the railways with a problem not only of recruitment but of morale, as senior railwaymen brought up in the old tradition found themselves working alongside younger men who were not prepared to accept the old conditions, and often felt no loyalty towards their seniors or towards their profession.

But right up to the end of the steam era, it seemed that every boy wanted to be an engine driver when he grew up. Most changed their minds before it was too late, but there were enough to provide the railways with the men they needed. The child viewing the grandeur and responsibility of the express train locomotive crew did not realize that he was looking not so much at an elite as at survivors, for of the hundreds of young men who each year joined the locomotive staff at the low level of engine cleaner only a small proportion ever reached the heights of a driver in the top link. Most fell by the wayside, some because they could not accept the prospect of long years messing about with oily rags inside cold and dirty locomotive sheds, others because their physique and especially their eyesight declined below the high standard that was required by railway service. Others never progressed beyond fireman, or perhaps driver of a shunting locomotive.

Such failure to obtain promotion was often less a matter of ability than of luck: if there were no vacancies there was no promotion.

In contrast to, say France, enginemen in Britain were expected to learn on the job. Whereas an aspiring French locomotive man would be expected to study the theoretical side of locomotive construction and operation, the corresponding British worker would, by long years spent performing tasks beneath his ability, develop an intuitive feel for locomotives that was invaluable and could hardly be acquired in any other way. The British way enabled men of little formal education to rise slowly to positions of skill and responsibility, but it meant years of drudgery which some of the brighter individuals could not accept. It was only after years spent as a cleaner, then as a passed cleaner (cleaner/fireman), then as a fireman and passed fireman (fireman qualified to drive) that a man might become a driver, first of a shunting locomotive, then of a freight engine (where, probably, the highest degree of skill was required). Finally, and if he was lucky, and probably when he was not far from retiring age, a locomotive man could acquire the status, dignity, and paypacket of a passenger train driver.

The years spent firing were the most taxing. The most common reason for losing time (and falling behind a train's schedule was a reportable misfortune that could lead to a reprimand) was the inability of a locomotive's boiler to provide the steam that was required. A fireman could bring about this sad situation by lack of skill; different types of engine (and to some extent different types of driver) required different methods of firing, different in terms of frequency and the placing of the shovel-loads. Failure to feed the boiler with fresh water at the most suitable times could lead to the same result, and there was always the possibility of inferior coal adding another negative factor. The physical skill involved in heaving several tons of coal into a small hole on a bucking footplate was soon acquired by a man of reasonable physique, but the ability to cope with run-down engines, poor coal, and sometimes unpleasant or unhelpful drivers was a real test of brain and experience.

But although life was more satisfying for an express train driver, it was hardly more comfortable. He was still subject to call-out in the middle of the night or, more usually, in the small hours. (Calling out was one of the jobs of the cleaners, and it was not a pleasant job. The right address had to be found in the dark, and its unwilling and sometimes bad-tempered occupants had to be roused without, if possible, waking the neighbors and inviting a flow of invective or, occasionally, missiles). The driver would turn up at the locomotive shed complete with tea-can and meal-box. He would sign on, read the notices for any announcements of mishaps, track repairs, and changes that might affect the running of his train. He would then join with his fireman to seek his engine. The latter would already have its fire burning, and the fireman would tend it so that a full head of steam would be available at departure time. Both the driver and fireman would examine the engine for any possible faults, and the driver would see to the lubrication. If the locomotive had not already been coaled and watered the crew would take it to the appropriate tracks for these services, and would then await the signal to proceed out of the shed yard to the departure tracks.

Both driver and fireman would be totally familiar with their route; at night they would be able to orientate themselves simply by the changing pattern of sound. Both were responsible for observing signals; in fact, some signals were so placed that the fireman's side of the cab was the best place to watch for them. Few engines had speedometers, but drivers' experience and their pocket-watches enabled them to observe schedules without exceeding speed limits. Trains ran according to working timetables which, unlike the public passenger timetables, provided passing times for stations at which there were no scheduled stops.

No trip was quite like another. There were so many variable circumstances that the number of permutations was countless: the state of the engine, of the coal, of the weather, the load behind the engine, unexpected delays. The skill of a driver could be gauged by how consistently he could cope with such variations to achieve an on-time arrival. It was always possible to 'thrash' an engine (and its fireman) by driving harder than was economical, achieving high horsepower but only at the expense of excessive coal consumption and repair costs. This was not regarded as good practice, except perhaps on railways that had a policy of providing engines that were too small for some of their tasks.

Once the trip was finished, the enginemen would take the locomotive to the engine shed and hand it over to the shed staff. They had the unpleasant task of clearing out the soot from the smokebox and raking out the firegrate and ashpan. The latter was a particularly nasty job, as it was performed while the engine was still hot and usually entailed the hard labour of breaking up clinker. Ash disposal was another chore, and most locomotive depots faced the problem of finding somewhere to put the ash. An equally dirty job was coaling the engines. Typically an elevated stage was used, whose denizens shoveled coal from wagons into trolleys that were then tipped into a locomotive's tender. In the last decades of steam, tall concrete coaling towers that lifted coal wagons bodily upward in order to tip their contents into a storage

Above: *During a stop at Salisbury enginemen shovel the coal forward, to make the fireman's work easier. Coal of similar poor quality was often supplied in the 1950s.*

Left: *A music hall song emphasizing the dangers and responsibilities of the railwayman's work.*

Upper right: *One of the nineteenth century patent locking frames that made it harder for a signalman to make a mistake.*

Lower right: *Operating semaphore signals towards the end of the steam age.*

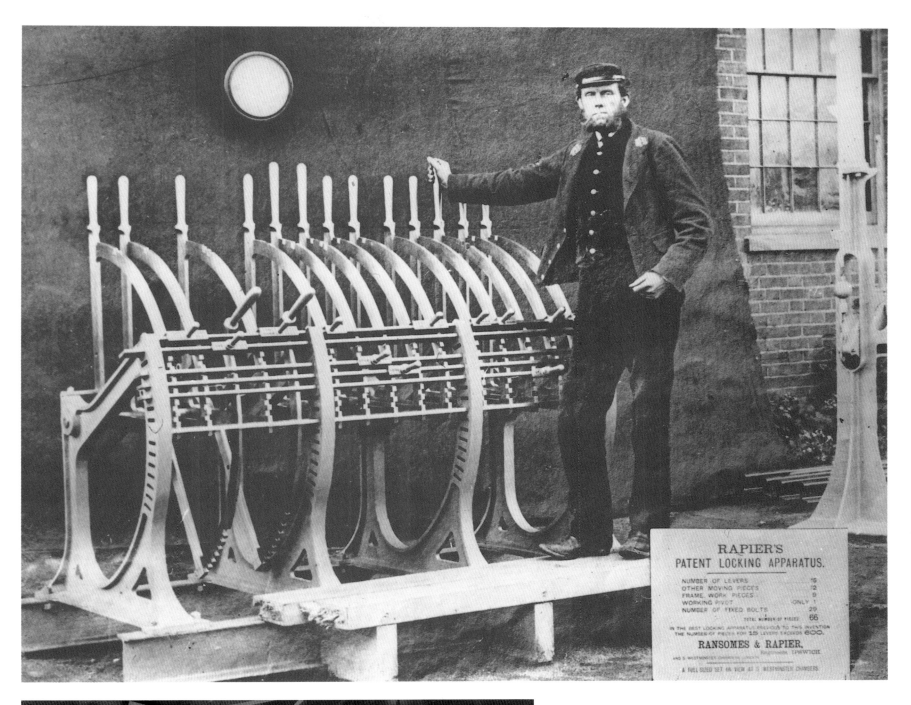

RAPIER'S
PATENT LOCKING APPARATUS.

NUMBER OF LEVERS   15
OTHER MOVING PIECES   12
FRAME, WORK PIECES   9
WORKING PIVOT   ONLY 1
NUMBER OF FIXED BOLTS   29

TOTAL NUMBER OF PIECES   66

IN THE BEST LOCKING APPARATUS PREVIOUS TO THIS INVENTION
THE NUMBER OF PIECES FOR 15 LEVERS EXCEEDS 600.

RANSOMES & RAPIER,
Engineers IPSWICH.

AND 5 WESTMINSTER CHAMBERS LONDON

A FULL SIZED SET ON VIEW AT 5 WESTMINSTER CHAMBERS

hopper, were occasionally provided, and these did make coaling a less barbarous job.

Where trips were short, locomotive men might take back another train, or they would return to their home shed as passengers ('on the cushions'). On the longer runs they had to rest at the destination before taking back another train the next day or the next night. These so-called lodging turns were not popular because, whether the stay was spent with a family that took lodgers or in a railway hostel, it was certainly not like being at home.

For most, becoming a top-link driver was the limit of ambition. It was possible to speed promotion by applying for transfers to depots where there were vacancies. With the coming of British Railways in 1948 an engineman could apply for a posting to any depot in the country and thereby leap ahead of his stay-at-home fellows. It was also possible, given the right ability, to become a locomotive inspector, whose job was to keep a check on footplate crews and both monitor and aid their promotion. Respon-

Left: *Ballast packing, a frequent job for permanent way workers.*

sible positions in locomotive sheds were filled from a variety of sources. The top position, shedmaster, was usually occupied by an engineer, but the shed foreman on most railways could be a former driver, although this position was usually reached through the grades of mechanics and fitters.

Enginemen, perhaps more than other grades in the railway industry, were also involved in voluntary work. Many took first-aid courses, while senior men helped with the Mutual Improvement classes. The latter were organized to teach men to pass the examinations that were a prerequisite for passing from cleaner to fireman and from fireman to driver. In particular, an intimate knowledge of the quite complex rule-book was required.

Among other operating staff the signalmen occupied a special place. Partly because they were isolated in their signalboxes, partly because they did not handle money, they were less supervized than other grades. Indeed, one of their traditional tasks had been to oversee others, and they were supposed to inspect passing trains to ensure that everything was in order and that enginemen were working according to regulations. Although their prime task was to ensure safety, they had an important decision-making role because whenever a train fell behind its schedule it was the signalmen who rearranged the sequence of trains so that as few as possible would be held up by the late-running service. In the later decades, on busier routes, some of this

decision-making was shifted to district control systems, where a central office coordinated the planning of train movements and telegraphed its instructions down the line to the signalmen. Working to a system of bell codes passing information from box to box, pulling the heavy point and signal levers, recording the passage of trains, the signalman could be overworked at peak periods and one of the first things he learned was when to make the tea.

With responsibility for life and limb just as obvious as the signalman's, the permanent way worker had a less stressful life. Indeed, the life of the lengthman was close to the ideal for an outdoor job. It was regular and responsible, but not rigidly programed. Within limits, the lengthman could take his own time. His main duty was to walk over the sector of track that was his responsibility, checking for alignment, repacking loose ballast, noticing any faults that might be developing, and hammering back the keys (wedges) that had fallen out from their position between rail and chair. Lengthmen formed part of a permanent way gang, consisting of a ganger and a handful of lengthmen who worked together on some tasks. Their headquarters was the platelayers' hut. These simple structures, familiar lineside objects placed at regular intervals, were traditionally built of old sleepers, but in later years some were of brick. The Southern Railway, which because it had its own concrete works tried to make everything possible out of concrete, built concrete

Right: *Platform staff attend the departure of a cross-country train from Oxford.*

Below: *A major job of relaying on the L& Y at Bolton in 1914.*

huts that have survived into modern times. The platelayers' hut was where tools were kept, where tea was brewed, and from where, in foggy weather, the permanent way staff were deployed to operate the fog warnings, detonators placed on the rail beside signals at danger.

Another permanent way gang, much larger, was concerned with reballasting and rail replacement. Reballasting involved removing the old ballast, cleaning some of it and disposing of the rest, and introducing new ballast. Until the introduction of machinery late in the steam age, this was a shovel

job, and muscle power was the main factor in re-placing rails and sleepers. Teams would be given possession of a line at night or on a Sunday to carry out this work. Their trains were typically provided with messing, and sometimes sleeping, vehicles and would move from place to place on a railway division according to demand.

Men working together as gangs had lookout men, armed with a brass bugle, to warn of approaching trains. Lengthmen working alone did not have this security, nor in those days did they wear high-visibility clothing, but they developed a sixth sense which reinforced their knowledge of the timetable. But this was not infallible; in 1904 a tardy permanent way man was said to have interrupted the record-breaking run of the GWR *City of Truro*. After yard shunters, permanent way staff had the highest casualty rate of all railwaymen. On average, one or two were killed each week on the British railways, although this declined to a little more than one in the 1940s, despite war conditions. Not all the casualties were run down; bottles flung out of fast trains by un-caring passengers could be lethal.

Station workers were either salaried or non-salaried (an important social distinction since it determined whether a person was regarded as working class or not). The lower ranks of the clerical staff were the lower ranks of the salaried staff, and began with junior male clerks and then went upwards through six classes of senior male clerks. Female clerks, who became quite numerous in the 1940s, were non-salaried.

Non-salaried station staff began at the porter grade, and from that grade a competent man, given luck, could rise to other operating grades including signalman, ticket collector, guard, stationmaster and, occasionally, higher management. The station porter, whether he was a passenger or freight porter, had a variety of jobs. Some were unpleasant, like cleaning the station lavatories, and others were agreeable, like tending the station gardens, but there was the common factor that the porter was constantly at beck and call. When a train was in a station the porters had to be on hand to answer passengers' questions, help them enter or leave the train, carry their baggage, help load the parcels van, help with prams, check all doors, signal to the guard that the train was ready to leave, and if necessary pursue a departing train down the platform to secure a door-handle.

Promotion to guard brought fresh responsibilities, but only a small wage rise. Starting as a freight train guard, the new entrant learned to move around inside his brakevan without being hurled to the floor or on to some hard object by the sudden jerks of the vehicle. As guard, he was responsible for the train's paperwork, which was considerable because each vehicle and consignment was documented and it was the guard's duty to see that each consignment or car was delivered to its proper destination. He was also responsible for operating the brake of his vehicle, which on most trains was the only brake on the train, apart from the locomotive brake, that could be operated while the train was running. Ex-

Left: *A Southern Railway brakevan.*

Above: Handling London's milk in the 1890s.

perience taught him when braking was needed, but he was always ready to screw down his brake in response to a whistle signal from the driver. After the rough, hectic, and sometimes bruised existence of a freight guard, promotion to passenger guard was like entry to heaven. It demanded a smarter uniform, a more cultivated language, perhaps equal patience, and brought greater prestige and more contact with people.

Among station staff the stationmaster was dis-

tinctive both in terms of dignity and function. This was reflected in his uniform, which had more gold braid than anybody else's and was usually newer and better cut. He was responsible for anything that happened at or near his station, both passenger and freight, and he needed to be knowledgable in order to keep an eye on things. Under him were the uniformed and non-uniformed staff (a distinction close to that between salaried and non-salaried, the chief non-uniformed personnel being ticket and freight

clerks). He had to see all messages that came to the station, whether by telegraph or by train-pouch. He also needed to be something of a salesman and public relations expert, taking an interest in the clientele and always finding time for a chat.

The stationmaster was answerable to a line or regional office, which was where contact was made with the managerial echelons. Railway managers were traditionally found from the lower ranks, among men who were ambitious and highly competent although, as elsewhere, there were too many cases of ambition alone being enough to reach these heights. In general, there was little intelligent preparation of managerial staff. Men who rose from the ranks tended to know their own particular speciality but needed to learn, if they could, the other aspects of railway service, and even then too many of them lacked the habit of thinking objectively. But if future managers had been taken from intelligent school-leavers there would have been a danger of appointing men who were clever but lacked a real understanding of the railway business. One railway which did tackle this problem was the North Eastern, with its Traffic Apprentices Scheme. This took graduates and other intellectually qualified people and employed them at successive spells in all the railway departments, so that by the time they took managerial positions they were capable of tackling, or at least understanding, all possible railway jobs. This scheme was continued by the LNER and was eventually adopted by British Railways as well. In this way the railways finally obtained a degree of managerial competence, placing them ahead of much of British industry.

The top of the promotion ladder was the post of general manager. Holders of this position were far more influential and important than heads of departments, even though in later years chief mechanical engineers attracted more public attention. Although it was not unknown for engineers to reach the position of general manager, this was unusual, and chief mechanical engineers and chief civil engineers were considered to have reached the pinnacle of their professional life. Locomotive engineers usually began as premium apprentices. They were from families wealthy enough to provide them with a suitable schooling and then pay the premium to the chief mechanical engineer whose pupil they would become for a number of years, mixing practical labor

Top: *A line-up of GWR officials as the last broad-gauge train prepares to leave Paddington in 1892.*

Above: *The crew of a 'Schools' locomotive with a minute to spare before departing from Waterloo Station in 1937.*

Right: Advanced facilities at Southend in 1938. The former Great Eastern 4-6-0 has just coaled at the overhead plant and is being turned on a powered turntable in readiness for its next working.

Below: Murky working conditions at the GWR Worcester locomotive depot.

Overleaf: A Malayan Railway 4-6-2 approaches Tumpat. The locomotive is one of the final batch built in the 1940s.

in the workshops with theoretical study in their spare time; it was a busy life that was not only unpaid but, in fact, bought. However, once they successfully terminated their apprenticeship they had brighter prospects. They were often sent away as shedmasters, but might well return to the main works to specialize in production engineering or design work for both locomotives and rolling stock. This was the path followed by most of the chief mechanical engineers this century, many of whom served more than one railway in the course of their lay careers.

By its nature, the railway service was one of the most dangerous. Its essence was active machinery, and it was forced to operate at night, in fog and snow, and to maintain a schedule regardless of conditions. Over the years the casualty rate slowly declined, as did accidents to passengers, but they were nevertheless high. In the early 1940s, the railwaymen averaged five accidental deaths per week. A quarter of these were track workers, but the most dangerous trade was that of the freightyard shunters, who had to run alongside moving freightcars to apply brakes or to use their poles to attach and detach the chain couplings.

Yet until the mid-1940s the profession of railwayman was much sought-after. Those who did not have the right connections were often rejected, a situation very different from the earlier years of railways, when the demand for skilled or literate workers made the companies less discriminating in their selection, and from the postwar years when higher wages and faster advancement made factory work more attractive.

Left: *The LNWR compound locomotive* Queen Empress *is shipped for exhibition at the Chicago World Fair.*

Lower left: *Builder's photograph of a 4-8-2 built by North British for the Natal Government Railways.*

Below: *An Atlantic locomotive built by North British for the North Western Railway of India in 1907.*

A popular railway book of 1910 was called *Our Home Railways,* and for decades the financial columns of the serious newspapers had a section called 'Home Railways.' This was a necessary term, because it would have been ambiguous to refer to 'British Railway Companies' when so many overseas railways were owned and operated by British firms.

When other countries followed the British example and built their own railways, it was only natural that they should call on British experience. They hired British engineers who, in turn and quite rationally, recommended that they should import the equipment from Britain rather than attempt to build it at home. As the decades passed this British predominance weakened. Some countries developed their own style and design, while others set up their own workshops. But in many parts of the world the British tradition was retained, providing a market for the railway supply industry and rapid promotion for trained emigrants. In these countries the railway scene closely followed British example. Shorn of their cowcatchers and commodious cabs, the locomotives of India, Africa and South America not only resembled each other but also the engines to be seen on Britain's home railways. The British semaphor signal, too, was a kind of trade mark advertising the British connection.

In the railway world, the British sphere of influence did not coincide precisely with the British Empire. Canada right from the start chose to follow US examples, which was a natural choice since both countries faced the same physical problems. New Zealand by the end of the century contrived simultaneously to follow British, US, and its own home-grown styles. It could design and build its own locomotives but frequently had recourse to British and US builders. For many years Holland, (which far from being part of the British Empire had an empire of its own) was a good customer of the British locomotive companies. Further afield, Argentina could be regarded as a honorary member of the Empire so far as its railways were concerned, for they were almost entirely British companies with their head offices in London. The same was true of India and, on a smaller scale, for most of the British colonies in Africa. South Africa also bought most of its locomotives in Britain, but exercised close control over their design. Australia was divided. Queensland developed its own style of railway; its locomotives, largely home-built, looked American, but its signals were pure British. The other Australian states were, visibly at least, in the British tradition.

The role of British specialists varied from country to country and from period to period. Most of these countries passed through a stage in which locomotive men came from Britain and in due course either went back, or became permanent settlers and progressed perhaps to higher ranks like locomotive inspector or locomotive depot foreman, while locally born men were trained as drivers. A similar picture was to be seen with engineers and managers, although the speed at which local men were trained to take over again varied considerably from country to country, and does not appear to have depended on how far the indigenous population was Anglo-Saxon, as might have been expected. Most engineers trained in Britain, then went overseas after being attracted by the better conditions and pay offered by the recruiting agencies in London.

Once there, they usually stayed to make a career, but there were many exceptions to this general rule. Overseas service could bring fast promotion and hence a quicker accumulation of experience, enabling a man to leapfrog ahead of his contempor-

aries at home and return to Britain to take a much better job. In modern times, the Southern Railway's chief mechanical engineer R.E.L. Maunsell was an example of this. He began as an apprentice in Dublin, then went to the Lancashire & Yorkshire Railway but soon took a job with the East Indian Railway, which advanced him to district locomotive superintendent. Within a few years he was back in Ireland as locomotive superintendent, well placed to become an influential locomotive engineer for the last quarter-century of his career. Barton Wright, who in the 1880s succeeded in bringing order to the L & Y locomotive department, was an interesting case, for he had formerly been locomotive super- intendent of the Madras Railway, and he chose to re- turn to India after his spell in Lancashire. The Wors- dell brothers, who designed locomotives for the North Eastern Railway, both spent several years with the Pennsylvania Railroad. Another NER engineer, Walter Smith, whose work did so much to make the 'Midland Compound' a success, had pre- viously spent nine years as locomotive super- intendent of the Japanese Government Railway.

That the Argentinian railways were British com- panies that merely happened to be physically dis- tant could not have been more strongly emphasized than when the Buenos Aires & Great Southern Rail- way (known as BAGS) began to build a new station in the capital: the personnage invited to lay the foundation stone was none other than the Prince of Wales, later the Duke of Windsor. The station was necessary to handle the intensive suburban service, which saw over 160 arrivals and 160 departures each working day. Some interesting three-cylinder 2-6-4 tank locomotives were imported from British builders for this service which, after Liverpool Street in London, was the world's biggest steam suburban service.

Like other large countries in which early railway building had been entrusted to Britons, the Argen- tine had a gauge problem, with four British-owned broad-gauge (5 foot 6 inch) companies, two standard-gauge, and one meter-gauge. In practice, because lines tended to converge on the capital and the ports, little through train running would have been attempted in any case and the gauge problem was not as enormous as it was in Australia. The BAGS was the largest of the Argentinian com-

Left: *Beyer Peacock locomotives still at work in New South Wales in the 1970s. The center locomotive is of a large class of 4-6-0s introduced in 1892.*

panies, owning about 850 locomotives in its busiest year, 1929, rising to a maximum of over 900 in 1932. It operated a fleet of very British-looking 4-6-0 passenger locomotives, many of which were named. The later 4-6-2s were also named, typically after Argentinian generals and birds. After naticnalization two new engines were named *General Peron* and *Eva Peron*, but were hurriedly renamed after the political upheaval of 1955.

These two locomotives belonged to a class of thirty delivered by the Vulcan Foundry in 1949 and were of the 4-8-0 wheel arrangement, a rarity for British locomotives. This wheel arrangement, however, was quite popular in the Argentine, and the Buenos Aires Western Railway had similar units.

They were mixed-traffic engines, and reflected the importance of fast freight trains in the Argentine, with its heavy seasonal meat and fruit traffic. The BAGS examples were designed precisely with the Rio Negro Valley fruit trains in mind. These moved 750 miles to the Buenos Aires docks at passenger-train speeds, and sometimes weighed as much as 2000 tons. The fruit traffic coincided with the summer holiday traffic peak, which meant that from about December to March the locomotive situation was very taut, and the mechanical departments were required to ensure that every possible locomotive was available during that period.

It was therefore an advantage that the Argentinian steam locomotives were of the robust if un-

Below: *A 3-cylinder 2-6-4 tank locomotive design supplied by three British builders to the Buenos Aires Great Southern Railway in the 1920s. This unit is hauling a suburban train into Buenos Aires.*

Right: *The former Eva Peron, a 4-8-0 supplied to the BAGSR in 1949 and intended mainly for fruit traffic.*

Below right: *British-built locomotives of the former BAGSR outside their depot at Buenos Aires in 1968.*

sophisticated design favored by British builders. Moreover, they had to remain in service for many years longer than their depreciation life. In fact, steam traction still survived in the Argentine at the beginning of the 1990s. After 1929 the railways lost much of their previous prosperity, with the devaluation of the Argentinian currency, new labour laws, and the prohibition of most tariff increases. New locomotives and rolling stock arrived in smaller numbers, which meant that old equipment remained in traffic. 80-year old locomotives were still working hard in the 1960s.

The Argentinian railways were nationalized in 1948. Some of the British staff stayed on for a few years but the railways' situation deteriorated in the face of even lower capital investment and politically-motivated idiocy. Argentinians had been groomed for high positions, but life was made difficult for them by the government and most of them left railway service, being replaced by less qualified personnel who, in many cases, were political appointees. The demoralization of the staff was especially regrettable because of the harmony that had been achieved during World War Two, when German and Italian immigrants continued to work amicably alongside the British. But despite their bad treatment the railways continued to function. Diesel locomotives were acquired but, at least in the early years, their reliability was such that steam traction was restored to several dieselized services.

Argentine's neighbors Uruguay and Paraguay had similar British-style systems, although that of Paraguay, which was simply a long singletrack line with a long branch, could hardly be called a system. A peculiarity of the Paraguayan state railway was the regularity with which announcements of its imminent reconstruction were made. On each occasion the anticipated investment was not forthcoming and the few trains continued to be hauled by the locomotives originally supplied for the line, supplemented by additional units acquired from the Argentine. Elsewhere in South America the British influence was weaker. Systems such as those of Chile and Bolivia did buy British locomotives, but the orders were shared with other countries. Thus the Argentine, Paraguay and Uruguay formed a British-style trio, and one of the many things they had in common was the practice of folding back a locomotive's leading buffers, so that collisions with errant cattle would be less messy.

The Indian railways had many similarities with the Argentinian, even though their political setting was very different. They also had their head offices in London and bought their locomotives in Britain. They, too, used British specialists, although these were replaced by local men rather sooner than on the Argentinian lines (in the 1920s the companies

Upper left: *A British-built 4-6-0 ekes out its last days in the Argentinian Andes.*

Lower left: *A Paraguayan State Railways train stops for a redistribution of wood fuel. The open car, in which extra logs are stored, is one of many items of British equipment on the line.*

Above right: *A British-built meter-gauge tank engine relegated to shunting at Oruro, Bolivia.*

Right: *One of the handsome 2-6-0 engines supplied by North British for the newly-built Paraguayan main line in 1910.*

agreed that three-quarters of the higher posts should go to Indians, although the qualifying examinations would still be conducted in English). The 5 foot 6 inch gauge was also the main Indian gauge, although there was an equivalent mileage of meter-gauge, as well as some narrow-gauge lines.

The Indian economic and social situation meant that in many ways British experience needed to be modified in order to conform. The caste system, interestingly enough, did not prevent passengers of different status traveling together in the lower classes, but vegetarianism did complicate railway catering. Because trains were slow and distances long, there was a big demand from those who could afford it for first class travel, with cool and spacious vehicles offering thief-proof sleeping and sitting accommodation, and with meals served inside the compartments. Europeans traveled first class not simply because of their social status but because they were physically not fitted for a tough life in Indian circumstances. In 1915 a British regiment that despatched a troop train without ice and cooling fans caused the deaths of 32 men from heatstroke.

Above: *Meter-gauge locomotives at Bangalore. At the left is one of the standard 0-6-0s of the 1880s while one of its replacements, a postwar 2-6-2, is on the right.*

Above left: *A special vice-regal train provided for Lady Curzon's 1902 visit to Hyderabad.*

Left: *A 4-6-0 built to British Engineering Standards Association specification for the Bombay Baroda and Central India Railway.*

Third class was very cheap but very cramped. Although Europeans were not prohibited from using it, they did not. It was not until after Indian independence that all the faster trains began to take third class passengers, and to redress the long-standing imbalance the first post-Independence government made a point of introducing 'Janata' trains, which carried third class passengers only, but on fast schedules. In British India the companies took some pride in the low fares that enabled the masses to undertake railway journeys, and there were the occasional fast trains, like the East Indian Railway's 'Howrah-Delhi Third Class Express,' which were designed for cheaper class passengers. But in general the provision of amenities for such passengers was so minimal as to approach the horrific, and too many railway workers and managers despised third class passengers. Symptomatic, perhaps, was the labeling of compartments for the exclusive use of women (in itself a considerate provision): lower class compartments were labeled 'Women Only,' whereas first class accommodation was 'Reserved for Ladies.'

Because the Indian railway network had been planned by government, there were few competing services. But the Great Indian Peninsula Railway and the Bombay Baroda & Central Indian Railway both had Bombay-Delhi routes, although the BBCI route was shorter and flatter than the GIP line. Despite this, there was a 'Race to Delhi' in 1927 between the boat trains that ran in connection with the weekly arrivals of the P&O service from England. The BBCI's 'Punjab Special' had no difficulty in doing this run in less than 24 hours, and the GIP boat train could not match this. With the normal fast trains on this route, the BBCI led with its 'Frontier Mail,' whose schedule for the 861 miles was brought down to 23 hours and 50 minutes, an overall average of 36 mph, which was better than it seemed in view of the lengthy station stops that were a necessity in India. The GIP's matching 'Punjab Mail' ran the 956 miles in 29 hours and 38 minutes, with 30 stops. World War Two, as in Britain, saw a regression and in 1946, the last year of British rule, the BBCI train was down to an average of 33 mph.

By that year the number of British staff was down to about 200, and they soon left. The new regime handled the railways intelligently and traffic rose steeply. In course of time the British-built locomotives were followed by those built in India or imported from countries offering low prices, but the British locomotives remained in secondary service and, indeed, can still be seen in the 1990s. British-

Above: *Bound for La Paz, a passenger train of the Bolivian State Railways picks its way through the market at Oruro, hauled by a 4-8-2 supplied in the 1950s.*

style semaphore signals also remained in service, being replaced by color lights on only a few modernized routes.

In 1965 Indian railways had about 80 different types of broad-gauge steam locomotive, 80 on the meter gauge, and about 50 on the narrow gauges; on the broad and meter gauges almost all traffic was handled by just a few classes, because locomotive standardization had been introduced quite early. Locomotive designs were closely related to what was happening in Britain and, as in Britain, by the end of the nineteenth century the 0-6-0 predominated for freight and the 4-4-0 for passenger services. But the broad-gauge North Western Railway had ordered some 4-6-0 freight locomotives in the 1880s, and from this design came the celebrated 'Jones Goods' locomotive of Britain's Highland Railway, an interesting example of 'colonial' practice influencing the home railways.

Most of the British locomotive builders sought orders from the Indian railways. It was a market in which the British had an advantage, but it was not

Right: A cross-frontier train at Amritsar, India, with Indian Railways British-built 4-4-0 and green Pakistan Railways passenger vehicles.

Above right: Broad gauge locomotives at Jamalpur, India. A typical British 0-6-0 is at left.

143

entirely closed to other countries. Sometimes when the British builders had full order books, locomotives of their design were built under license in other countries. On at least one occasion locomotives were ordered from the USA in order to put pressure on British makers. Also, there was a desire to provide a locomotive industry in India itself; the Ajmer Works of the BBCI produced meter-gauge locomotives to standard British designs for many years, and independence was followed by the founding of a new all-India locomotive works.

The British military authorities in India wanted locomotives that could be easily transferred from one railway to another in case of emergency, and the builders themselves were not averse to standardization. Accordingly in 1903 the British Engineering Standards Association (BESA) worked out designs for a standard series of locomotives to be bought by all the Indian companies. Technically, the main innovation of these essentially British-style designs was the provision of larger grates, because high-calorific British coal was being replaced by Bengal coal. Some of the BESA types are still to be seen on Indian Railways. The BESA broad-gauge 4-6-0, in fact, was still being imported in the 1950s. The different companies did specify, or instal, detail modifications for their BESA locomotives, but on the whole the standardization exercise achieved its aim.

After World War One, however, the railways decided that new types were desirable, in view of

heavier traffic and rising fuel bills. Wider fireboxes, capable of burning cheap coal, were needed. Accordingly, another standardization program was envisaged, while some railways began to order experimental locomotives. A committee evolved five new broad-gauge 'Indian Railway Standards' designs, but unfortunately reported too early to take into account the tests of experimental locomotives.

The committee, sitting in India, only made recommendations amounting to outline specifications. The final designs were made in Britain, with the Indian railways' consulting engineers, the BESA, and the builders all participating, together with just one engineer from India itself. The working drawings were not seen in India until after the engines were built, a situation that was quite usual and saved months of delay.

Railways all over the world from time to time found themselves using locomotives that, quite unexpectedly, turned out to be unsuited to the job. This happened in India with the new standard locomotives, although the failure was on such a scale as to be unmatched elsewhere, except in the USSR. In India, where a local press and legislature were flourishing, this affair ultimately became known as the 'Pacific Locomotive Scandal.'

The new locomotives, whose delivery began in 1926, were three 4-6-2 types, (the large XC, the medium XB and the small XA) and two freight 2-8-2 with the same standard boilers, the XD and the

Above: *A 4-6-0 of BESA specification supplied to several Indian railways in the 1950s.*

Upper right: *Outside Parel locomotive works in Bombay. One of the smaller (XC) version of the standard interwar Pacifics is on the right, overshadowed by the postwar US-style Pacific on the left.*

Right: *Indian narrow-gauge trains at Dabhoi. The locomotives are of a standard 2-6-2 design introduced in the 1920s.*

larger XE. Possibly because so many committees took part in their design, they turned out to be failures. The XB and XC had poor steam distribution and were very sluggish, while the XB boiler dimensions were obviously wrongheaded, the tube cross-sectional area being so small that the gases produced in the grate could not find a clear passage to the chimney. The Pacifics, in addition, had frequent frame fractures and tubeplate cracks. The time spent by these locomotives under repair meant that the old BESA units continued to perform the top duties.

Nevertheless, the locomotives continued in production and it was not until a number of fatal derailments aroused the government that any action was taken. A special investigating commission was summoned from Britain, and included Stanier, the chief mechanical engineer of the LMS, and a top civil engineer from the GWR. The committee carried out trials, and decided that some modifications needed to be made to the suspension, after which the locomotives could continue in service provided speedometers were fitted and they were subjected to speed restrictions. The incident reflected little credit on the Indian railways, which had continued to order locomotives that they knew to be defective, or on the British locomotive industry.

It was probably this experience that caused the Indian railways to entrust the design work of the postwar passenger locomotive to Baldwin in the USA. However, the corresponding freight design, the WG 2-8-2, was a typically British product, and

the first hundred units were built in Britain (one was exhibited at the 1951 Festival of Britain), before hundreds more were built in India. There was also a light 4-6-2, the WL, designed in Britain.

On the meter gauge, three new British-designed standard types were built between the wars, two designs of 4-6-2 and a freight 2-8-2. The postwar standard types of 4-6-2 and 2-8-2 were predominantly American in concept, but a useful 2-6-2 for secondary services was designed in Britain during the 1950s. This was the YL, of which many units were subsequently built for India in Hungary, Germany and Japan.

Pakistan's locomotive history was the same as India's until 1947. Subsequently, it did not introduce new designs but continued with the old locomotives, merely buying a few new units and hoping that dieselization would prevent a locomotive shortage. As in India, prewar steam locomotives remained in service in the 1990s.

In other parts of the British Empire the 3 foot 6 inch gauge was favored. This included South Africa, which had a highly-developed system of government railways whose locomotives and rolling stock were just as large as the standard-gauge trains of Britain. Locomotives were built in Britain but, rather than leaving design in the hands of consulting engineers in London, the SAR mechanical engineering department took a large role in the design process. David Hendrie, who became the first chief mechanical engineer of the newly constituted South African Railways in 1910, had been chief draughts-

Above: *One of the ill-fated XB Pacifics, demoted to slow train service, in this case suburban work at Madras in the 1970s.*

Left: *The standard Indian Railways broad-gauge 2-8-2 Earlier units were built by North British in 1950, but this example was made in India. No fewer than 2,450 engines of this class were built between 1950 and 1970.*

Right: *A Class 19D 4-8-2 locomotive leaves Oudtshoorn, South Africa. This class was supplied by North British in 1948 and was designed for branchline service.*

Above: *A Pacific sets off from Tumpat, terminus of the East Coast Line in Malaya, in 1972, four decades after the line was completed.*

Left: *One of the world's most distinguished stations, Kuala Lumpur in Malaya.*

man of the Highland Railway before emigrating. He designed his own 4-8-2, a wheel arrangement that was to become a South African favorite, and introduced to South Africa the Garratt locomotive, which also became a widespread type.

Other British systems in Africa were smaller. The Rhodesian railways followed the South African pattern, whereas further north the systems of East and West Africa took the form of lines from the ports into the interior. The East African Railways operated Garratts, but also conventional locomotive types, some of which were identical with those supplied to West African railways.

A very different system was that of the metergauge Federated Malay States Railways. Probably because it served a prosperous territory, this was a smartly-run railway, and at Kuala Lumpur had one of the world's most spectacular examples of station architecture. For most of the steam age this railway

Far left: *A YB metergauge 4-6-2, a type built in Britain from 1928. A handful were also built in India, including this locomotive.*

relied almost exclusively on successive versions of a 4-6-2 design for both freight and passenger work, the final classes being three-cylinder engines with Caprotti rotary valve gear, built by North British. Locomotives were named, with one nameplate in English and the other in local script.

Australia provided the most variety. The different states owned and supervised their own government railway systems, each in its own way. Victoria and neighboring South Australia both opted for the 'Irish' 5 foot 3 inch gauge, and these were the only adjacent states which, having the same gauge, could operate interstate trains. The 3 foot 6 inch systems of Queensland, Western Australia and Tasmania were far apart from each other, and New South Wales, which had taken the precaution in the early days of opting for the standard gauge, found itself odd-man-out after all, although standard gauge was later chosen for the federal Commonwealth Railway, linking eastern and western Australia across the Nullarbor Plain.

In the twentieth century Tasmania and Western Australia ordered British locomotives which in some cases were very similar to those supplied to the African colonies. The Western Australian Government Railways, almost completely re-equipped after World War Two, had brought its existing locomotive stock to the point of exhaustion. A class of 4-8-2 from Beyer Peacock and of 4-6-2 from North British were the mainstay of its services in the years before dieselization. The 4-8-2s were designed to burn the local Collie coal, having wide fireboxes, and also provided labor-saving features including self-clean-

ing smokeboxes and self-emptying ashpans. In Tasmania, where the railway system was small, the last class of locomotives, built by Robert Stephenson, were Pacifics that were almost identical with meter-gauge Indian locomotives built by the same company. They were also remarkable in that the entire class was saved for preservation after dieselization. The other 3 foot 6 inch system, Queensland Railways, soon abandoned its British traditions and built its own locomotives to US-influenced designs.

US influence also showed itself on the South Australian Railways between the wars, after the

Above: *A Victoria Railways pass of 1899, allowing free passage to a liner at nearby Port Melbourne.*

Left: *On the Western Australian Government Railways in about 1900, with a Perth-Kalgoorlie train. The locomotive was supplied by Dubs of Glasgow in the 1890s.*

Right: *One of Robinson's celebrated 'ROD' 2-8-0 locomotives which, after military service in World War One, was sold for colliery use in New South Wales.*

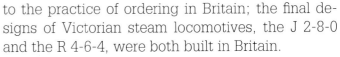

Below: *A Beyer Peacock 4-6-0, designed in 1891, at work on the New South Wales Government Railways in 1970.*

government appointed as railway commissioner a man whose previous job had been with a US company. Confronted with a stock of worn-out and small engines he decided to acquire big American-style locomotives. What precisely happened after this is uncertain, but the upshot was that designs prepared by the American Locomotive Company somehow found their way to Armstrong Whitworth in England, who constructed a series of plainly American locomotives for the SAR. In neighboring Victoria, there was a trend towards locally built engines, but after World War Two came a reversion to the practice of ordering in Britain; the final designs of Victorian steam locomotives, the J 2-8-0 and the R 4-6-4, were both built in Britain.

Most British of all in its locomotive policy was the New South Wales Government Railway. This railway bought its locomotives mainly from private builders in Britain, supplemented by local engineering firms (which typically supplied a proportion of each class ordered), although their design was strongly influenced by the railway's chief locomotive engineers. William Thow, who held this position from 1899 to 1911, was a former London & North Western man, and the NSWGR designs in this period tended to incorporate some LNWR features as well as those of the builders, Beyer Peacock. His simple and rugged 4-6-0, 2-8-0, and 4-6-4 tank engine designs remained in service until the 1970s. His successor, E. Lucy, had served on the GWR at Swindon Works, so it was not surprising that his first passenger locomotive had a GWR-style taper boiler and Stephenson valve gear. But probably most British of all were the 0-6-0 locomotives built from 1877 for freight service and which remained in service until the 1970s; these would have looked at home on any of the British railways.

Up in Queensland an interesting development took place in the cane fields. These had used specially-designed narrow-gauge locomotives built by John Fowler of Leeds, which were very successful. However, Fowler abandoned the locomotive business in 1938, and in order to maintain supply of its popular 0-6-2 tank locomotive the drawings were acquired by an engineering company in Queensland, which built a new batch in the 1950s.

Apart from the sugarcane companies, there were many other private railways in Australia, and

Left: *Another view of the Beyer Peacock 4-6-0, seen here hauling out of Newcastle the last regularly steam-hauled passenger train in New South Wales.*

Below: *A sugar-cane train in Queensland, hauled by a Fowler of Leeds locomotive, constructed locally.*

coal companies in New South Wales provided employment for several 2-8-0 locomotives of Great Central Railway design. These had been built for the Railway Operating Division of the British war department in World War One for services in France and, like many of their sister units, were sold off cheap at the end of the war. Some units found their way to China, and some to Australia.

Another class of British locomotive that was sent abroad for war service was the 'Dean' 0-6-0 of the GWR. In World War Two many of these were captured at the fall of France, and some found their way to other parts of German-occupied Europe. A few units ended their lives in China.

Indeed, in wartime the number of British railways abroad tended to increase in line with the fortunes of war. In World War One the lines from Calais and Boulogne to the British sector of the Western Front were under British control and showed an interesting combination of French and British practice. In the Middle East in World War Two many lines were operated by the Royal Engineers railway companies, which were virtually composed of railwaymen in uniform. The line from the Persian Gulf to the Soviet frontier was one of these. Many engines of Stanier's LMS 8F 2-8-0 type were sent to this region, and some of them were still working in Turkey 40 years later.

The glamorous years of British steam ended in September 1939, but there is some justice in the claim that its most remarkable years began precisely then. Under war conditions, some of the basic virtues of the steam locomotive became conspicuous, and particularly its ability, unmatched by more modern forms of traction, to function in the absence of proper maintenance and to operate with inferior fuels. These conditions of poor maintenance and inferior coal continued for some years after the war, but for two decades there was a kind of last fling, when the nationalized British Railways depended on steam traction to bring back the prewar standards. It was a period when smartly turned-out express locomotives worked alongside grimy run-down engines, leaking steam at every gland.

The users of the railways in those postwar years would have rejected the idea that the railways were offering anything as good as prewar standards. The stations were still shabby, looked uncared-for, and trains tended to be overcrowded and unpunctual. This impression of poor quality was joyously fostered by most of the press, so even when in the 1950s British Railways began to innovate, to provide new and better services, the improvement was not always noticed.

The spirit of the age impressed itself on the railways. With good labor hard to obtain, and good coal likewise, new locomotive designs tended to emphasize ease of maintenance and ability to thrive on inferior fuel. The age of the common man had arrived, or so it was said, and this meant that efforts were made not to improve the best facilities, but to multiply them so that they would be offered to more people. This was why in the 1950s there were as many named trains as before the war, even though they were not as outstanding in terms of comfort and speed as the prewar titled trains.

Nonstop long-distance trains were slow to be restored, although they did increase over their wartime numbers. In the last peacetime summer the companies had 18 services running nonstop for distances exceeding 170 miles. Most of these were on the LMS, but the LNER and GWR also had several, whereas the Southern Railway, with its mainly short distances and lack of water troughs on its long line to Devon, had none. These trains averaged from 47 mph to 68 mph, the two fastest being LNER services. By summer 1943 the total had declined to eight (or ten on Saturdays), and their speeds had fallen to the range of 41 to 49 mph. Two were on the GWR and the rest on the LMS. Yet these apparent declines masked a triumph in terms of locomotive performance, because loads were vastly increased; not only were wartime trains longer but they tended to be packed tight with sitting and standing passengers. There were occasions on the LNER main line out of Kings Cross when trains of no fewer than 24 coaches were despatched, hauled by the same locomotives that in peacetime had pulled the nine-coach 'Coronation.'

1939 was the last year when the railways had freedom to choose their investment objectives, and it was a freedom that they were never to regain; in the immediate postwar years they needed government sanction for obtaining raw materials, and after nationalization their investment intentions were scrutinized by civil servants anxious to keep railway

Top left: *An 'Austerity' 2-8-0 kept by the Royal Engineers for postwar training.*

Above: *War Department locomotives awaiting disposal in 1948. Most are 'Austerity' 2-8-0s, but there is also a requisitioned LBSCR 4-4-2 tank locomotive.*

Top right: *One of Bulleid's 'Merchant Navy' Pacifics after rebuilding by British Railways.*

Right: Lord Dowding, *one of Bulleid's light Pacifics, after rebuilding. The locomotive is hauling an Exeter train at Templecombe.*

Previous pages: *One of Stanier's '8F' 2-8-0s at work on the Western Region of British Railways in 1953.*

investment as low as possible, even of capital accumulated from railway revenues. Sometimes, as in the ill-judged conversion of locomotives to burn oil, the investment was against the judgment of railway managements, but was imposed by government. The postwar plans of the companies, which in retrospect seem rational and perceptive, had little chance of execution, and were eventually replaced by programs designed for the nationalized British Railways, plans which were far less sensible.

One of the problems was that the generals-fighting-the-last-war syndrome was very evident in the early years of British Railways, which took over the four companies at the beginning of 1948. The government, insofar as it had any detailed intentions at all, anticipated that railway nationalization would be best done according to the pattern of London Transport, a publicaly-owned enterprise that had earlier and very successfully taken over several metropolitan transport companies. So far as locomotives were concerned, policy was largely in the hands of former LMS engineers who, remembering that what had saved the LMS locomotive department from collapse in the early 1930s had been the prompt introduction of new designs by William Stanier, prescribed the same recipe for British railways two decades later. The result was a range of new steam locomotive types that were basically Stanier in inspiration, although with some changes to fit them for an age of scarce skilled labor and of inferior coal. The postwar railway company plans for locomotive modernization, which in fact were more progressive, were abandoned. For a time the company workshops were allowed to continue building prewar types, and in fact the Western Region of BR built new batches of 'Castles' and other 4-6-0s. But as the new standard designs came into production, the prewar designs were abandoned, as were some interesting postwar designs of the LNER.

Although during the war the railway works had been busy with munitions production, locomotive building had not ceased. There was a shortage of freight locomotives, and the LMS standard 8F 2-8-0 was built by several works and became a national standard. Meanwhile, in preparation for the re-occupation of continental Europe, locomotives designed for overseas service appeared. Some of these were American, but the British War Department ordered hundreds of a new design, the 'Austerity' 2-8-0, whose dimensions were similar to the Stanier 2-8-0 but was simpler to build and operate. A few 2-10-0 versions of this design were also built. When the war ended many War Department engines were available for civilian use. Some of them, like the old GWR Dean 0-6-0s that had been requisitioned in 1939, were soon scrapped, but the 2-8-0 soon became a familiar sight on the British railways.

Right: *One of a batch of GWR 'Castles' built after the war. Swansea Castle leaves Leamington Spa in 1950.*

Left: Calcutta, *an old run-down locomotive still in service in 1948. This 4-4-0 was of the GWR mixed-traffic 'Bulldog' class, built in Edwardian times.*

Below: *Christmas traffic in a militarized Britain.*

There had also been the building of so-called mixed-traffic locomotives by the Southern Railway. These turned out to be the big 'Merchant Navy' passenger engines, 4-6-2s designed by Bulleid and incorporating many original features, including chain-operated valve gear, oil-bath lubrication, disc driving wheels and an 'air-smoothed' exterior. Not all these features worked out well in practice, but because the boilers produced ample steam the work of these Pacific locomotives was, for the SR, revolutionary. A scaled-down version, the 'West Country' type, was also in production by the end of the war. These locomotives would hardly be described as 'austerity,' but Bulleid did create another locomotive that took wartime economy to extremes. This was his Q1 0-6-0, in which everything that was not functional was sacrificed. It was a capable design, even if its boiler did look as though it had been made from cardboard boxes. With Bulleid the desire to innovate was obsessive, and his good ideas tended to be obscured by his bad ones. After he had left the SR most of his 4-6-2s were rebuilt, with their air-smoothing and other undesired features removed. His final fling on the SR had been his 'Leader' design, a steam locomotive running on powered bogies. This was soon abandoned.

The Bulleid 4-6-2s had what, for Britain, was a record high boiler pressure (280 psi, as compared to the 180-250 psi current in other designs). This pressure was also a feature of the new 4-6-0 introduced on the GWR at the end of the war, the 'County' class. A two-cylinder design with driving wheels intermediate between the 6 feet of the 'Halls' and the 6

foot 8 inches of the 'Kings,' it was said to be intended mainly for the hilly main line in Devon, but it showed no great improvement over existing types, which continued to be built. Meanwhile the GWR finally abandoned the familiar outline of its shunting engines, six-wheel locomotives with square ('pannier') tanks and tall domes and chimneys. The new 9400 class had a tapered domeless boiler and a smaller chimney. It was little different from its predecessors, but at least it looked less old-fashioned.

Above: *More War Department locomotives awaiting disposal in 1948. These were former GWR 0-6-0s that had been requisitioned for foreign service in 1939.*

Left: *Stanier Class '5' engines continued to be built after the war. This example, photographed at Bromsgrove in 1949, was designed experimentally with Caprotti rotary cam valve gear.*

Right: *A Bulleid light Pacific in its original form, on the 'Golden Arrow' at London Victoria.*

Below: *One of the standard BR locomotive designs. This is a 2-6-4 tank engine, very similar to those designed by Stanier for the LMS before the war.*

A certain Americanization could be witnessed on the LMS. With labor shortages, the British railways had the same need for labor-saving designs as the US railroads had long experienced. Easy access to the running gear was one requirement, easy cleaning was another. Self-cleaning smokeboxes (in which a grid broke ash and soot into particles that would be exhausted out of the chimney) and easily shaken grates were features of this philosophy. A large and small 2-6-0 design, and a tank engine version of the smaller of these, included these features, but in addition the LMS continued to build Stanier designs, sometimes modified in detail; the 2-6-4 tank locomotives, for example, were deprived of part of their footplating to save weight. Existing streamlined 4-6-2s lost their streamlining, which was considered inappropriate for an era of not very fast trains and added to labor costs, while further examples continued to be built in an unstreamlined form, with the later examples having roller bearings. The LMS also experimented with different kinds of valve gear on its Class 5 4-6-0, whose production continued.

On the LNER, locomotive design underwent a great change after the death of Gresley in 1941. His successor, Edward Thompson, was a former North Eastern man who gave the impression that he did not approve of the Gresley concepts. This distrust had some justification insofar as the refined Gresley valve gear, an essential part of his three-cylinder designs, showed itself to be very vulnerable in wartime conditions. Thompson's first move was to rebuild Gresley's *Cock o' the North* with conventional valve gear and 4-6-2 wheel arrangement. He also rebuilt Gresley's first Pacific with conventional valve gear, and this became the basis for a series of Pacifics built by Thompson and his successor, the A1 and A2 types, the former with 6 feet 8 inch driving wheels and the latter with 6 foot 2 inch. Thompson's ideal was a two-cylinder locomotive with careful balancing that would enable balance weights to be held to a minimum. Over 400 of his B1 4-6-0, designed on these principles, were built and performed quite

Above: Batchelor's Button, *one of the A2 3-cylinder 4-6-2 class introduced by the LNER in 1947. It is shown leaving Thornton Junction with an Edinburgh-Aberdeen train.*

well as mixed-traffic locomotives. The K1 2-6-0, rebuilt by Thompson from a Gresley design and subsequently adopted as a standard type, was essentially a scaled-down version of the B1, while the L1 was a tank engine variant of the latter. On the whole, the LNER postwar designs were less exciting than the Gresley types but were better adapted to an age of austerity.

While company designs, old and new, were being built, the new British Railways mechanical engineering department planned the introduction of new designs. As a preliminary move it was decided to try out existing company designs on a scientific basic, hauling a dynamometer car for measuring performance and with each design operating on the lines not only of its original company but of the others as well. In this way, it was said, it would be possible to select design features that would be suitable for locomotives intended for service over the whole country. In principle, an express passenger, a mixed-traffic and a freight locomotive were taken from each of the previous companies' stock and tried out on their own and three other lines. In reality, there were some exceptions; GWR locomotives were too wide to operate on lines other than those of the parent company and the LNER, and the SR was represented by only its two types of 4-6-2. A good time was had by all, but the force of the conclusions was weakened by the circumstance that the locomotive crews had received different instructions on how to drive. Some emphasized fuel economy, some did everything to make up for lost time, while others dutifully observed the sectional timings laid down even if they were behind time. The GWR representatives, with their low superheat, were disappointing in terms of coal and water consumption, although otherwise their performance was good. The Gresley streamlined Pacific and the Stanier 'Rebuilt Scot' did well, the Stanier 'Duchess' not so well, but the sheer energy of the two SR Pacifics was impressive even though their fuel consumption was not. On the whole, the tests did more for railway enthusiasts than for locomotive design.

The member of the Railway Executive responsible for mechanical engineering (that is, the chief mechanical engineer of British Railways) was R.A. Riddles, a former LNWR engineer who had continued with the LMS and had helped design the Stanier range of locomotives. During war service he had designed the 'Austerity' locomotives. He believed, rationally enough, that British Railways would eventually electrify, but until that time came steam traction would dominate. He did not anticipate the mass, ill thought-out, dieselization program of the 1960s which condemned many of his steam locomotives to very short lives. Insofar as his ideas for the future were more rational than the policy actually followed, it is wrong to accuse him of

Right: A B1 'Antelope' 4-6-0 of the LNER. This is Madoqua *at Louth in 1950.*

sponsoring a range of unnecessary locomotives. That he followed LMS practice in his new designs is unsurprising, given his background and that of so many of his assistants, although it is arguable that the locomotives introduced by BR showed little advance over those of the old companies. Only one was outstandingly different.

There were 12 designs in the new range of so-called 'BR Standards.' For ease of construction and maintenance they were two-cylinder designs, and they were intended to thrive on poor coal. There were three designs of 4-6-2 (heavy, medium, and light), two of 4-6-0, three of 2-6-0, two of 2-6-2 tank, one of 2-6-4 tank and finally and most innovative, a heavy freight locomotive that was intended to be a 2-8-2 but finally emerged as a very successful 2-10-0.

The medium Pacific, *Britannia*, was the first to emerge, and 55 were eventually built. This was a competent design, and when it was drafted to the Great Eastern main line it was possible to introduce a vastly accelerated schedule between London, Norwich, and other East Anglian points. Other units

Above: *A Gresley A4 Pacific, Kingfisher, at Aberdeen in 1966.*

Left: *The conventional blastpipe, as used by the great majority of British locomotives, designed in an era of cheap coal.*

Above: *A Leeds train at Bradford Exchange in 1967. The locomotive is a 2-6-4 tank of modified Stanier design introduced by the LMS in 1945.*

were sent to help out on the Western Region, and handled London – South Wales trains. In smaller numbers they were used for other services, including the 'Golden Arrow.' The small Pacific was the 'Clan' class, which was a small 'Britannia' with the same 6 foot 2 inch driving wheels but suitable for use on lines that could not accept a heavier engine. Only ten were built, and they were used in Scotland, proving useful on the former Glasgow & South Western line. The large Pacific, *Duke of Gloucester*, was the only unit of its class. It was a more innovative design and used Caprotti rotary valve gear. The latter was theoretically more efficient than conventional types, but difficult to apply to steam locomotives. Unfortunately, any advantage it might have provided was obscured by poor steaming, a deficiency that was later attributed to a mistake made during construction at Crewe.

The larger of the two 4-6-0 designs was simply an update of the Stanier Class 5, with driving wheels two inches larger, and was just as capable. Eventually, it would total 172 units, more than any other of the BR standard designs, apart from the 2-10-0. The

lighter version, for use on lines with weight restrictions, was also a competent design. Of the 2-6-0 types the smaller and medium versions were derived from similar LMS designs, while the larger was the least necessary of the BR designs. It weighed a mere two tons more than the medium type, enabling a slightly higher boiler pressure to be used. The smaller variant formed the basis for a lightweight 2-6-2 tank locomotive, which was supplemented by a slightly larger tank locomotive of the same wheel arrangement. The 2-6-4 tank was more numerous than either of these, and could be regarded as the final flowering of the Stanier 2-6-4 tank introduced in the 1930s.

Much more enterprising was the freight 2-10-0, of which more than 250 examples were built, and of which No.92220 was destined to be the last steam locomotive built for BR. Ten coupled wheels were unusual for Britain; hitherto there had been the 0-10-0 'Lickey Banker' built by the Midland Railway, and 25 'Austerity' 2-10-0s acquired by the railways after the war. The new locomotive was a powerful machine with 5 foot driving wheels, and it soon

settled down to heavy freight work. Moreover, its balancing was so good that it could run at high speeds, and in the holiday season it was often used for passenger trains. Three units were fitted with mechanical stokers, another innovation for Britain, but these were found to be of no great advantage. Others were fitted with the Italian 'Crosti' boiler, which had a separate water space for preheating the water. This, again, was found not to be worth the extra expense. The later units were fitted with double chimneys, benefiting from a technical development that had begun before the war.

The importance of a smooth, powerful, exhaust as a means of providing a firm draught for the fire had long been recognized; on it depended not only the rate at which steam was produced, but also the complete combustion of the coal. Prewar practice in France, where wide chimneys and double chimneys produced good results, had been observed in Britain. Some of Maunsell's locomotives had been provided with wide chimneys, Gresley used double chimneys on some of his streamlined Pacifics, and the double chimney provided for the 'Rebuilt Scots' was regarded as an important reason for their enhanced performance. The GWR had been a little slower to experiment, the basic excellence of its designs having lured it into complacency. But even the

Far left: *A GWR 'Castle' restarts the 'Cornishman' after the line has been cleared by sidetracking a freight 'wrong line' and parking a 'Hall' on a divergent line.*

Left: *The British Railways title is applied to an LMS 'Jubilee' soon after nationalisation in 1948.*

Below: *The 'Scarborough Flyer', hauled by a pair of Gresley's 'Hunt' class 4-4-0s, at Malton in 1951.*

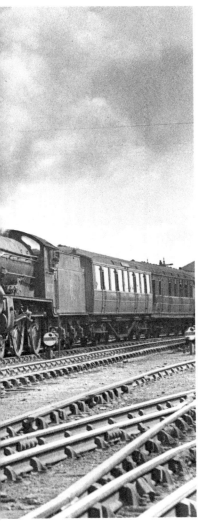

Great Western tried out the double chimney on the first of its new 'County' class engines and, after becoming the Western Region of BR, it continued to experiment. Double chimneys were fitted to some of the 'Castles,' and to all of the 'Counties' and 'Kings.' The performance of the latter in their last years was notably better than when they were new because of this improvement. The researchers at Swindon, by persistent experimentation, also discovered that precise adjustment of the blastpipe, which exhausts steam up through the chimney, was crucial. Among results that were claimed was a doubling of maximum steaming limits for the GWR 'Manor' class 4-6-0 and the LNER V2 2-6-2.

The 'Kings' were destined to be one of the last heavy passenger locomotive types to remain in the service for which they had been designed; while other lines being dieselized or electrified they continued to run from London to Birmingham and Wolverhampton until 1962. But it was the Southern Region which operated the last regular mainline steam passenger trains, its Bournemouth trains being served by Bulleid's Pacifics almost up to the end of British steam traction.

In the 1950s Southern and Western region passenger locomotives were turned out smartly for the better trains, and indeed some trains reverted to

their old company liveries. Most BR passenger locomotives were painted in a variation of the GWR's Brunswick green livery, although for a time the most powerful passenger locomotives bore a colour resembling the blue of the old Caledonian Railway. Mixed-traffic locomotives were black with decorative gilt lining, while freight engines were plain black. In the final years of steam traction, engine cleaning was neglected, so most locomotives were simply a grimy black. This external condition was a true reflection of their mechanical state, and the sight and sound of poorly maintained locomotives, swathed in leaking steam and emitting knocks and whines from their mechanism, became all too common.

Postwar recovery of train services began with the Southern Railway and ended with suburban and freight services, where the change was less a question of restoring services than of bringing the rolling stock back to prewar standards. On the SR, cross-channel boat trains had restarted even before the war ended, partly because the government saw such trains as a visible reassurance to liberated France that things were getting back to normal. The 'Golden Arrow,' however, was not restored until 1946, and the 'Night Ferry' in 1947. Because the SR had not been a high-speed railway, the wartime speed restrictions had hardly affected its schedules, and accordingly it had little difficulty in returning to prewar speeds.

In 1947 the SR actually introduced a new train, the 'Devon Belle.' This was a Pullman train designed for holidaymakers, and had sections for Plymouth and Ilfracombe. It had an observation car at the rear, an unusual feature for Britain although the LNER 'Silver Jubilee' had offered one in the last prewar summers. The 'Devon Belle' was also claimed to be non-stop between London and Exeter, but in fact changed engines at a secluded station just west of Salisbury. The new and restored SR named trains were usually hauled by Bulleid's Pacifics, whose designer was also busy creating new passenger vehicles. Ever reluctant to perpetrate the normal, Bulleid managed to build a handful of windowless buffet cars, which he called tavern cars, embellished with fake half-timber and brick side panels, but the weight of public ridicule soon put an end to these. After nationalization the SR carried on very much as before. The prewar 'Atlantic Coast Express,' with its numerous sections detached at West Country junctions en route, was accelerated thanks to the Bulleid Pacifics and in 1961, its peak year, was scheduled to run the 84 miles from London to Salisbury in 80 minutes, which was quite good for such a heavy train.

On the Western Region, the former GWR, the 'Cheltenham Flyer' did not reappear after the war,

Left: Earl of Clancarty, *a GWR 'Castle,' in BR service at Bristol in the 1950s.*

Below: *Another 'Castle' with a London-South Wales train in BR maroon and cream livery.*

Right: *A BR 2-6-4 tank locomotive still in service on a preserved steam railway.*

but another prewar train, the 'Bristolian,' was reinstated and became the Region's crack train. In the late 1950s, with 'Castle' traction, it returned to the prewar timing of 105 minutes, an average speed of 67 mph, and on one occasion it did the trip in a record-breaking 94 minutes. The 'Cornish Riviera Limited' also reappeared, and in fact differed little from the prewar train. It still left Paddington at 10.30 a.m. behind a 'King,' changing to a smaller engine at Plymouth for the final miles to Penzance. A less celebrated prewar train, the 'Cambrian Coast Express' from London to Aberystwyth, was also restored, and for its passage from Shrewsbury through the hills to the coast was provided with a modern 'Manor' 4-6-0 in place of the previous 4-4-0, enabling its schedule to be reduced to six and a quarter hours. On the London-Birmingham section it restored the prewar timing of two hours.

On the LMS the 'Royal Scot' had continued to run during the war, although it was then a heavier

and slower train. In 1952 it was still taking eight hours for its London-Glasgow run, although by then it had been reequipped with new rolling stock. The 'Flying Scotsman' of the LNER had a similar history. It, too, continued to run during the war, frequently with over 20 coaches but no restaurant car; an eight hour schedule between London and Edinburgh was achieved in 1945 and ten years later it was back to seven hours.

Elsewhere on the LMS, schedules were slow to regain the prewar level, and punctuality was consistently poor. This was partly because trains were longer, and really too heavy for the locomotives. On the Derby-Bristol main line, for example, elderly 'Midland Compounds' had to handle trains that were twice the weight of those they had hauled in their younger days. The LMS, and its successor the London Midland Region, also had problems of morale. Because of its prewar situation, when efficiency drives had resulted in ill-feeling, the LMS ob-

tained less company loyalty from its workers than the other companies, and this affected its performance in the difficult postwar years. Much of its territory was in the industrial regions, where labor problems were most acute, and this made the situation worse.

The two-hour services from London to Birmingham reappeared only in the 1950s, when it was possible to allocate 'Royal Scot' locomotives to the service. The GWR route to Birmingham reintroduced the same schedule at about the same time. These two routes were hardly competitive even before nationalization. Since the war years, return tickets issued by either company had been valid for both routes, and with nationalization competition was meant to disappear automatically. Nevertheless, it would seem that here, as elsewhere, company rivalries lived on for many years after nationalization. The Western Region had a harder task on this route, for even though it had powerful 'King' class locomotives for its 13-coach trains, the climbs through the Chilterns and up Hatton Bank were serious handicaps.

Pullman services had been withdrawn during the war, but the SR restored its 'Bournemouth Belle' in 1946. With 4-6-2 locomotives available, it could

Upper left: *A GWR 'King' storms Hatton Bank with a London-Birkenhead train in 1950.*

Left: *The 'Night Ferry' passes Folkestone in 1948, hauled by the light Bulleid Pacific Biggin Hill.*

Above: *The Swansea-London 'Red Dragon' in 1951, behind a 'Castle' displaying its train reporting number, a GWR innovation to make life easier for the signalmen.*

weigh over 500 tons on summer weekends. On the former LNER the 'Queen of Scots' was restored in 1952, although it was subsequently renamed the 'White Rose' and reduced to a London-Harrogate run. In 1948 a completely new Pullman service was introduced, the 'Tees-Tyne Pullman,' which provided a popular businessman's service between London and Newcastle. On the former GWR, which had previously not shown great enthusiasm for Pullman services, the 'South Wales Pullman' appeared in 1955. This ran between London and Swansea, and consisted of eight of the Pullman Company's oldest vehicles but nevertheless became popular among business travelers.

Many newly named trains began to circulate in the postwar years. Some of them were quite unexceptional, and appeared to have been given titles simply to make them seem special. This was not necessarily a foolish policy. It was good for public relations in the cities served by the new trains, and both the clientele and the operators did tend to regard a train as outstanding if it bore a name. In a sense, the new named trains were self-fulfilling prophecies, and did tend to become cleaner and more punctual than ordinary services. Among them were the 'Master Cutler,' introduced over the former Great Central route between London and Sheffield, the 'Inter-City,' over the Western Region's London-Wolverhampton route and providing an additional two-hour service for Birmingham, and the 'Capitals United' between London and Cardiff. Also serving the London to South Wales route was the 'Pembroke Coast Express,' which was one of the fastest of the new trains, covering the 133 miles to Newport in 128 minutes. On the former LMS, the new 'Midlander' from London to Birmingham covered the 94 miles to

Coventry in 94 minutes. Another train over the Great Central line was the 'South Yorkshireman.' Like the 'Master Cutler,' it was hauled not by an express locomotive but by one of the mixed-traffic B1 type, a sure sign that it was not regarded as a high-speed service. Similarly, the 'Saint Mungo' operated by the Scottish Region was regularly hauled by one of the BR standard mixed-traffic 4-6-0s.

Modest objectives in terms of average speeds would remain a characteristic of British Railways services up to the end of steam traction. Only with the introduction of diesel and electric traction, and the marketing of 'Inter-City (a brand name borrowed from the Western Region's train of the same name) did high speed again figure as an objective of passenger train planners. This change was not always smooth. After the 'Bristolian' was dieselized, a schedule based on the record-breaking run by a 'Castle' was introduced, but the diesel could not keep it and it was soon decelerated.

Right: *The LNER* Flying Scotsman *in excursion service in the 1980s.*

Below: *Another locomotive preserved for excursion service, the SR Pacific* City of Wells.

Bottom: *A 'Grange' 4-6-0, having hauled the 'Pembroke Coast Express' eastwards as far as Swansea High Street, prepares to back out of that station.*

INDEX

Acknowledgments

The publishers and authors would like to thank the designer Adrian Hodgkins, and the editor Judith Millidge for their help in compiling this book. We are also grateful to the following individuals and agencies for permission to use the pictures on the pages noted below.

Mrs V Johnstone Battye Library: page 150(bottom).
Birmingham Reference Library: page 35(bottom).
Bison Picture Library: pages 28-29, 30-31, 138(top).
British Library: page 140(top).
Colour-Rail: page 23(top).
Chris Gammel: page 10.
Hulton Picture Company: pages 21, 36, 48, 59(both), 64(top), 119(top), 120, 132(top), 167.
Mansell Collection: pages 49, 52.
National Railway Museum, York: pages 8, 9(top), 10-11(both), 12, 13(both), 16-17, 18-19, 20, 22, 30, 35(top), 38(all 4), 39, 42(top 2), 43(bottom), 44-45, 46-47, 53(all 3), 54(both), 60-61, 62(top), 65(bottom), 68-69, 76(bottom), 92(bottom), 100, 114-115, 116(both), 117, 118(top), 121, 123(both), 124(top), 125, 127, 128(bottom), 154-155, 158(bottom), 159, 166(top), 170(bottom), 171.
Peter Newark's Historical Pictures: page 43
John Westwood: pages 22-23, 24(both), 25, 34(middle), 41(both), 42(top), 43(top), 56-57, 58(top & bottom), 62(bottom), 64(bottom), 65(top), 66-67, 68(top), 69(top), 71(top 2), 72, 72(both), 74, 75, 76(top), 77, 80(both), 81, 84, 85, 86-87(both), 89, 90(bottom), 94(top), 95, 96, 97(bottom), 98, 99, 101(both), 104(both), 105(both), 106, 107(both), 108(both), 109(both), 110-111, 112(both), 113(both), 118(bottom), 119, 121(top), 125(top), 129(both), 130-131, 133, 134-135, 136-137(all 3), 138(both), 139(both), 140-141, 141(top), 142-143(all 3), 144, 145(both), 146-147(all 3), 148-149(all 3), 151(both), 152-153(both), 156(top 2), 157(bottom), 158(top), 160(both), 161(both), 162-163(both), 164(bottom), 166(bottom), 168, 170(top), 172(bottom).
Jim Winkley: pages 1, 2-3, 4-5, 6-7, 18, 19(top), 26-27, 27(top), 50(bottom 2), 51(all 3), 54(bottom right), 55(both), 58(middle), 63, 70(both), 78-79(both), 82(both), 83, 90(top), 91, 102, 103(both), 110(top), 111(top), 126, 157, 164(top), 169, 172(top), 173.